DAVI



# UNCONVENTIONAL GUIDE TO A BEAUTIFUL LIFE

HOW TO LIVE YOUR BEST LIFE, ENHANCE HAPPINESS, AND DISCOVER YOUR PURPOSE

*Unconventional Guide to a Beautiful Life*



First Edition 2024

Cover and Formatting: Streetlight Graphics

eBook ISBN: 979-8-9910416-0-7
Paperback ISBN: 979-8-9910416-1-4

# TABLE OF CONTENTS

**Introduction** 1

**Part I:
Finding the Source of Unhappiness**

Walking Your Own Path 7

Living In a Routine Cloud of Unhappiness 14

Social Programming 18

**Part II:
Understanding Yourself and the Universe's Energy**

The Ego and the Mind 33

Consciousness 38

Intuition 45

Vibration 54

Painbody 60

Karma 67

## Part III:
## Finding Your Path to Happiness


Designing Your Life 79

True Freedom 88

Getting Out of the Fog 97

Controlling Your Ego 101

Not Fighting Your Ego 106

Living Your Life Consciously and Artistically 109

Comfort Zones 114

Decision Making 119

Relationships 124

Relationship Foundations 132

Breakups 139

Gratitude 144

Energy Efficiency 149

The Importance of Nature 154

Spa For the Soul – Meditation 159

Acknowledgements 165

# INTRODUCTION

How to live a beautiful and happy life? This is a simple question. We all want a happy life, but as we all know, it's hard to create, achieve, and experience. This book provides alternative ways and ideas to finding and achieving happiness, and creating a truly beautiful life.

I have spent my career being a serial business entrepreneur. I have enjoyed building businesses from the ground up and have had the good fortune of success, allowing me to live my life mostly on my own terms.

Coming from a problematic, poverty-stricken, and challenging childhood, I have always had the feeling that there is more to life beyond the physical aspects and goals we are all chasing. When I was trying to understand the purpose of my life and the best way to design and live it, I found that many of the regular concepts people live their lives by did not bring me any closer to understanding the purpose of my life. More importantly, they did not bring me closer to finding happiness. Despite reaching financial success and freedom, having a family, and enjoying all kinds of social activities, practicing many hobbies and sports, and doing a significant amount of travel, none of it provided a continuous and uninterrupted flow of happiness. Enjoying these things only provided short glimpses of physical and mental satisfaction that disappeared quickly. The rest of my time was spent in a continuous routine of day-to-day tasks and dealing with various life challenges and emergencies.

So, I dug deeper, and by doing so, I have discovered that my life can be so much more beautiful, fruitful, interesting, and happy, if I am able connect to the energy flow of the universe and design my life aligned to that flow and on my own terms. I will be explaining the meaning of this and how to do it throughout this book.

When I was searching for my path to happiness, I discovered that I had to de-program myself from all the social programming our modern society imposes on us. There are many reasons for people not being able to find their happiness. Most people living conventional lives are not able to unlock their own path of happiness, as we are programmed to follow society's pre-programmed path of life. This pre-programmed social path might not be the right path for all of us. In fact, it is probably the right path for very few people. Some people feel various levels of satisfaction while their life trajectory is improving, but once they reach a certain peak, they start a steady decline in life quality again. Once people have reached the peak of their careers, their energy and enthusiasm for life can stagnate or deteriorate. The same happens when people reach the peak of their family lives or relationships. When the kids are all grown up and don't need them anymore, people lose interest in life. The same occurs when people reach the peak of various sports activities or hobbies. All of this leads to a decrease in happiness and harmony.

As I continued to grow and self-develop, I discovered ways to make my life beautiful, fulfilling, connected, and happy. More importantly, there was no peak and a slow decent in the quality of my life. On the contrary, the quality of my life is constantly improving. This includes my physical condition, mastering new skills, discovering new sports, participating in new experiences, having better and more beautiful relationships, improving in business, and, most importantly, increasing my happiness. I learned to enjoy the splendors of my physical life while following energetic and karmic life purposes, goals, direction, and connection. I discovered how to live life to its fullest potential.

This book is comprised of experiences and ideas of my last thirty years of self-growth and development. I have spent endless hours reading, thinking, meditating, studying, connecting, learning from mistakes, and talking with many people about life. Over the years, I have been asking and answering questions about the best way to live life. I found that the people around me asked the same questions and experienced the same struggle to find harmony and happiness. During those numerous conversations, I noticed a lack of practical knowledge or guidance in finding happiness while maximizing quality of life. We are missing the tools we could use in our day-to-day lives to improve our careers, businesses, relationships, and families, and general quality and happiness of our lives.

All this invested time allowed me to build the concepts that made my life amazing. I realized that all this knowledge exists and has been available for thousands of years, but a lot of people can't connect to it. Many of these concepts written and thought about in the traditional Eastern teachings are philosophical and hard to translate to day-to-day modern life. Therefore, the ideas in this book were meant to be an interface between our modern lives and the deep philosophical wisdom developed over thousands of years. None of the basic wisdom in this book is new—it has been accumulated and discussed in various philosophies over thousands of years. It has been written about in many books. The new formulations and ideas in this book were developed through a unique set of circumstances - my life. I discovered my life's purpose. I connected to the universe's energy. I found my path to happiness.

Now, in this book, I will share the ideas and concepts I have developed to make my life great, with the hope that those reading this book will use the concepts and ideas to make their lives great as well. Everything is written from the standpoint of how to make your life better, find internal harmony and happiness, and live life to its fullest potential.

I invite you to start the journey. Make your life beautiful and happy.

# PART I: FINDING THE SOURCE OF UNHAPPINESS

# WALKING YOUR OWN PATH

In today's society, we are programmed with a specific way we *should* live our lives. The programming begins right from birth, by our parents and extended family who show and tell us the way we should live our lives. This continues in kindergarten, grade school, university, and into the workplace. Essentially every person we are in contact with throughout our lives teaches us to follow a carefully scripted pattern. While some social rules, like not harming others, allow society to function properly and safely, other social rules strongly encourage us to structure our personal lives in a very certain and specific way.

Throughout kindergarten and grade school we are taught to behave in a certain acceptable way—a standard and average for the society we live in. We are not taught to develop our personal freedom, creativity, or personality. Then we are programmed to go to certain universities to study degrees considered popular in our society, even if that education won't lead us to a career that makes us happy to wake up every morning. After school, we are programmed to marry specific types of partners and have a certain number of children by a set age. While the numbers may differ slightly depending on the country and culture we are born into, the structure remains the same. We are taught to work a certain number of hours per day, go on vacation for a preapproved number of days, and retire at a certain age. Furthermore, we are even programmed how to spend our leisure time and what should make us happy and satisfied with our lives.

We are all programmed to do the same things at the same time and in the same way. This is called *social programming*. Most people follow social programming without a conscious thought. It just seems the only thing to do based on the endless programming received since birth. We mindlessly follow because we've been imprinted and programmed this way.

**The issue with the unconscious following of social programming is that in most cases it has nothing to do with finding our own happiness.**

The first step to finding happiness is to understand whether you are living a life that makes you happy or a life that was programmed into you by society. While there is a chance that a socially programmed life might make you happy, for the majority of people, this is not the case. You can verify this statement for yourself. Ask yourself the question, am I happy? Am I living my best life? Am I in harmony with myself and others? You can also look around you, and ask yourself are the people in your close circle happy, in harmony and living their best lives? You can take a look at the divorce rates. How many married couples around you are unhappy with their relationships? How many people jump out of bed with extreme joy, excited to go to work every morning? You can look at the percentage of people resorting to alcohol and drug use to temporarily escape unhappiness. You can look at people around you and see how many of them are genuinely healthy and happy. Most importantly, look in the mirror. Do you feel genuine harmony and happiness in your life?

Most people have structured their lives—in at least one aspect but usually in many aspects—based on these social rules and programs and not based on what works for them and what would make them happy. Most people, at some point, find themselves unhappy with their lives or at least with several aspects of their lives. As always, the first step in solving a problem is to be aware there is one. Is your life based on the social programming blueprint, or have you structured your life based on a blueprint you thought would make you happy regardless of social programming?

Once you accept that your life does not need to follow the same path as everyone around you, you can start imagining and designing what works for you. *What works for you* can be a confusing premise. What does that entail? The simple answer: you have the freedom to do what sparks and unlocks your internal happiness.

Some might think that walking your own path might create issues with the people who have been part of your programming, like parents, teachers, friends, and partners. While there may be truth to this, at the end of the day, only you are responsible for your happiness. No one can do it for you. You need to choose what is more important: living a happy life or satisfying someone else's wishes and ideas for you.

In reality, when you are happy, everyone around you will feel it and be part of that happiness. If someone is holding you back, then you have three choices. Give up your happiness to satisfy their idea of what is good for you. Follow your path to happiness despite the obstacles, and hope the relationship continues. Surround yourself with people who support your path to happiness. Only you can make these decisions.

In my case, it was a combination of the last two. My parents were programmed people who were not looking to do personal development. All their advice and direction were based on social programming. When I realized that in order to find my happiness I needed to find my own path in life, I had a lot of explaining to do. While I loved them, I had to do what worked for me. They continuously tried to make me follow their advice, even after I made it clear it was not relevant to me, so it took some time for them to understand and accept that I was determined to design and build my own life structure and find my happiness. Of course, they continued to try give me advice, based on their own programmed life concepts. But once I had a clear idea of what path I had to follow to design my life and find my happiness, I didn't let my parents contradicting advice derail me from that path. Eventually they realized my path made me happy, and they accepted my decisions. Furthermore, as they noticed the quality of my life, they even started asking for advice on how to find *their* happiness. I was more than happy to share my ideas with them.

My parents weren't the only people in my life following social programming. I discovered that many of my friends were stuck in the same predicament. Of course, I didn't realize it until I started developing myself. When I started doing this, I was able to see clearly how the people around me affected my life. In my twenties, I had a good friend. We travelled together, went out together, and did various projects together. We were inseparable. As the years went by, I took an interest in self-development. I strove for happiness, but my friend was blocked by social programming and didn't look for happiness outside of it. The relationship continued despite us having less and less things of value to share with each other. I didn't know what to do. We shared history and many years of connection, but the relationship no longer offered positive value for me. Eventually, after one of our regular phone calls, I asked myself, *what positive value does this relationship add to my life?* The answer was: *nothing.* This was the last conversation we ever had. In this case, I understood that despite the mutual history and past experiences, this relationship did not continue to add positive value to my life. From that day on, I decided to surround myself only with people who bring positive value to my life, and I to theirs.

People who choose to walk a different path in life can experience conflict between what they feel is the right path to happiness, and what society expects from them. Conflicts arise when people refuse to conform to social programming, and these conflicts can oftentimes cause stress and unhappiness. Both are a waste of energy. This type of stress is caused because we feel that we need to comply to all the social programming we have received during our lifetimes. But once we truly understand that we are free to choose our own life design and find our own path to happiness (as long as we are not harming others), there is no more conflict. The understanding of our own freedom of choice shows us that there is no point in wasting our energy on conflicts that do not improve our life quality.

**The true objective of our lives is to evolve and grow, to improve and unlock our internal happiness and our connection to the universe. We should be completely free to follow where our true happiness lies.**

You may be thinking, *how do I know the correct path for me?* The answer is simple. If you are happy, truly happy, whether based on social programming or not, you are living the correct life design for you. However, if you are not happy, change is needed.

If you don't feel the inner peace, happiness and harmony you crave, ask what is keeping you from finding this. Maybe you have not found it because you were looking for it only in the confines of your current comfort zone and the programmed life structure? Revisiting this assumption could allow you to understand that looking outside of your current comfort zone and outside of the programming you have received, might allow you to find your true purpose and happiness. A genuine feeling of happiness results from reaching your connection with the universe's energy—as will be explained in the next chapters. Through this, you will find self-improvement, growth, and evolution fall into place. What dissolves are the conflicts you once faced.

Free yourself from worry or concern that your life does not correspond with socially imprinted programming. What other people or society thinks is less important. Instead, focus on your path of self-growth to inner happiness and harmony.

# LIVING IN A ROUTINE CLOUD OF UNHAPPINESS

Most people in the modern busy societies live their lives surrounded by a cloud of routine, and this cloud of routine usually feels like negative grey or black energy. In the best-case scenario, it's just grey, neutral, slightly negative. In the worst-case scenario, people are surrounded by negative blackish energy. Obviously, it is not positive for our happiness and life quality to be surrounded by negative energy. So, why does this happen?

When we go through our normal day-to-day lives, we live in a state of routine. The routine itself is not a bad thing. The problem is that most routines consist of negative emotions—some small and some big. An example of a routine negative emotion is being upset at the traffic on your way to and from work. Others include being upset at your partner for not throwing the garbage out, being messy, or reacting to your kids when they are not behaving. How did you feel when your boss yelled at you, you were not promoted, or your friends did something you didn't like? Continuous conflicts in our work place or in our homes will generate a continuous flow of negative emotions, which in turn will generate negative energy around us, whether we are aware of it or not.

When we move through our day-to-day tasks, we do not notice all these negative emotions. But these small and big negative emotions accumulate inside our auras, creating a thick cloud of negative energy. The more we are unconscious of this accumulation of negative energy, the denser it becomes. We become accustomed to its presence.

What is the issue if we are used to living inside such a fog?

First, like living in an area with toxic air quality, our bodies and minds will not feel good when living surrounded by negative energy. Most people cannot identify the source of the problem, but they will feel unhappy, anxious, impatient, irritated, or afraid. Some try external stimulations and distractions to feel better, like love affairs, drinking alcohol, drug abuse, gambling, or partying. The purpose of these distractions is to escape the persistent negative feelings, but these distractions only offer temporary relief. In fact, distractions usually make negative energy denser—especially alcohol and drug use. Until the cause of the problem is discovered and dealt with, the accumulation of the negative energy will continue, and the negative feeling will not go away.

The second problem with living inside a negative energy cloud is that it blocks you from connecting with your soul and the energy of the universe. When one lives disconnected from their soul, there is no feeling of purpose and true happiness. Since it is difficult to see through a cloud of negative energy, some people get deeper and deeper into their shells. This intensifies and creates a black cloud that disconnects people completely from the universe's positive energy that exists everywhere beyond their cloud. The cloud becomes a cocoon, and living constantly in this type of negative cloud makes people tired, upset, depressed, and in some cases, suicidal. These negative clouds are obviously not good for our health or happiness.

So, how does one get out of their negative cloud?

The first step is to understand what is happening to you, or, more accurately, what is happening inside of you. Once you understand the negative cloud exists, and you notice the various negative feelings related to this, you can take action to dissolve the cloud. Maybe you notice the following:

- You feel constant negativity and negative emotions in your life
- You feel blocked from positive light and not feeling happy
- You are feeling tired, upset, depressed, or anxious

By noticing these various negative feelings, you can start doing something about it. It's a very important step to see the negative thoughts and emotions inside yourself. This is especially hard when those around you live inside negative clouds as well. People lose the ability to clearly see their situation. But once you step out of the cloud to see the situation for what it is, you have already done half of the work. Just stepping out and seeing the cloud of negativity around you will help you do something about it. You can start the process of clearing your aura—the energy field that surrounds your body.

# SOCIAL PROGRAMMING

Social programming dictates that every person in society should follow the same path, which is a curious notion if we consider that we are all different, and for each one of us to be happy, a completely different life structure and experience is required.

So why are we all following the same path instead of creating our life structure to achieve personal happiness? The answer is simple, and it is *social programming*.

When we are born, we are totally connected to our intuition. We know what makes us happy and are blissfully unaware of social programming. Kids know intuitively what games to play, and which activities result in happiness. We do not teach young children to connect with their intuition and we do not teach them to be happy. They are connected automatically, and they are happy automatically because of that. This is also one of the main reasons we connect to, and admire, young children: we sense their connection to the universe's energy and happiness, and we vaguely remember the feeling. We clearly understand we have lost those abilities and therefore enjoy seeing and feeling it secondhand in young children.

From the first second a child enters the physical world; we start indoctrinating them with our concepts of how they should live their lives. Parents indoctrinate and program kids with their ideas of the world—which is almost always some version of social programming—then schoolteachers do the same with their version of social programming. University professors continue the same cycle along with friends and extended family. But all this indoctrination and programming is based on ideas that were created by someone else.

For what purpose?

Over the last several thousand years, the rulers of society have figured out that in order to control the population, people must follow a defined set of rules that allow them to identify with the society they live in. When everyone follows the same rules, it is very hard to live outside the norm. Social pressure ensures that everyone will spend their lives doing the same things and following the same rules and structures. Furthermore, when living by the same set of rules, people identify with the institutions that created these rules and structures: religious institutions, governments, nations, clans, etc.

The main concept to understand here is that modern civilizations have developed over thousands of years into functioning societies with many rules, concepts, institutions, and commonly accepted ideas. While this structure contributed to the financial and physical progress of the general population, individual happiness has been largely ignored.

Our personal happiness does not advance the progress of society. And that is why it has not been the focus of society. Although social structures, rules, and accepted ideas do not contribute to happiness, living in a functional society with financial and social security is very important. Yet, why not add to it living in personal happiness and harmony? It's important to note that finding personal happiness and harmony—even if we need to search outside of social programming—does not contradict social prosperity. On the contrary. The more people living their lives in harmony and happiness, the more prosperous, productive, and conflict-free society will be.

Societies exist because of the social contract between individuals and their governments, whether it's a city, country, nation, state, clan, etc. The social contract between an individual and their country states the country provides security and services to the individual while the individual pays taxes and follows the rules and laws of society. This means the individual is guaranteed physical security, like a police force protecting property from criminals or military protection from foreign threats. In return, the individual pays for these safety benefits through taxes.

So, what is the problem?

The issue is that this social type of programming does not only exist on the general society level in order to keep societies functioning, but it also exists on an individual level in our personal lives. While programming on the society level allows people to function largely without issues, the programming on an individual level does not help us find personal happiness. The end result is unhappy people in a functioning society.

Look at your upbringing. From a young age, have you been doing things based on what you were told is good and proper based on the structures of the society you live in. How many people you know are living their lives based on what makes them happy? How many people have consciously structured their lives around happiness versus what their parents, teachers, and friends told them is right? This is not to say that parents, teachers, and friends do not want the best for us, they mostly do. But they are stuck in the same cycle, living their lives based on social programming. This is a simple example of the blind leading the blind.

The evolution of this is simple. Consider how most young children before the age of eight are free and happy—notwithstanding specific situations. Kids do not need advice on how to be happy. This happens naturally, because they are directly connected to their intuition. Adults force social norms and programming onto kids, and they believe us because they are small, and we are big. Parents, teachers, and family are authority figures. Over their childhood, kids have no choice but to start disconnecting from their intuition and happiness and connecting to social programmed structures and concepts that make them miserable. Society has succeeded in turning perfectly happy, free, and intuitive kids into miserable functioning adults.

Let's look at social convention programming from a spiritual angle. When a child is born, he is totally happy—because he is completely connected to the beautiful energy of the universe. He follows his intuition because this is the only thing he knows how to do. But as time goes by, the child starts to receive more and more information, more and more programming from the surrounding world. None of this programming directs the kid to continue following his connection to the universe's energy. Instead, he is shown societal patterns that were created to make society function in a certain way. As this process continues and the child's programming accumulates, his operating system—like a computer's CPU—changes from a universal energy operating system that is aligned with the universe and its energy, resulting in happiness, to a societal operating system which is basically a set of structures and life designs to allow the individual to function in the society, but have nothing to do with individual happiness. The child gradually forgets how to be connected and happy until the connection is gone. The soul and intuition fall asleep.

Again, there is nothing wrong with rules and laws. They are imperative to establishing and maintaining a functioning society. Consider the following social constructs, and what civilizations would be like without them:

- Do not kill
- Do not steal
- Do not harm others
- Respect ownership and fellow humans

Without rules and laws, there would be chaos. If a society does not have rules and laws that govern the general behaviours of people to provide safety and security to its inhabitants, there will be a low probability of finding personal happiness. Therefore, a functioning society, based on defined rules and laws that guarantees every participant's safety, is crucial.

What we are discussing here is the structure of life on an individual level. Societal rules and laws do not contradict basic intuition. The problem is structuring your life based on other people's ideas without examining what is right for you—your happiness and where your intuition is leading you. Should you be a lawyer or doctor because you love these professions? Or are you making choices because your parents expect you to be one or the other, or because both are considered great professions in society? Should you marry and have kids because doing so brings you joy and happiness, or because everyone else you know is getting married and having kids and it's socially accepted and expected from people your age? Are you pursuing paths only to discover your personal happiness lies in a completely different direction?

So, what is the alternative? As discussed earlier, the first step is to understand that we are all unique, with different intuitions, and specific needs. What is intuition? Religions and philosophies define intuition in different ways, but for me, it's simple. Intuition is our soul talking to us. Now, *soul* is a big word. It is used and defined in many ways by different philosophies, but for me, again, it is simple. We *are* our souls. If you ask me, who am I, I can tell you who I am not. I am not my body. I am not my brain. I am not my job or profession. I am not my role in the social structure around me, like father, husband, son, or grandfather. Those roles are part of me and my experiences in the world. But they are not the essence of me. I am the energy inside of me, this energy is my soul. This energy never dies. This energy wants to connect to all the energies inside other people and the energy of the universe, creating harmony and love. I will expand on these ideas in the following chapters.

This sounds easy, but it's not. Because in most people, this energy is blocked. Blocked by what? Social programming!

We are all born totally connected to our souls—the beautiful universe energy within us. But then our parents and society teach and program us in their ways, separating us from our inner selves. Slowly, we forget how it feels to connect with our inner energy. We forget how to listen to our intuition which is our inner energy (our souls) trying to speak to us. By the time we are teenagers we are completely disconnected from ourselves and all we know is to follow what everybody else is doing and thinking—following social programming. By doing so, not only do we forget our purpose on this planet, but we forget how to be happy. By the time we are adults all we know are the routines that keep us functioning in society, while many of us spend our whole lives fluctuating though various levels of misery with only slight and very brief glimpses of happiness.

Is anyone truly happy all the time? If most of the population is disconnected from their inner selves, what about the minority who are not? These are people who, for some reason, despite being subjected to social programming throughout their lives, can connect to their inner selves, their souls, through their intuition. While the how and why are unclear (to me), I suspect these people have *old souls*, and these old souls have past life experiences that emerge through the blockages created by social programming.

Once you have felt that shine of happiness, even for the briefest moment, it is impossible to ignore. You will start searching—I call it *walking the path*. There are endless paths you can follow to your inner self—your soul's energy inside you and the connection to the universe's energy and splendor all around you. While on this path, you will feel the shine of true happiness. I am not talking about the happiness you feel when you buy a new car or a new designer bag; this feeling will fade away in a matter of hours, days, or less. I am talking about true happiness from the inside, the universe's light that shines through your inner self. You feel your soul through your intuition, and the resulting happiness is eternal and unstoppable. It doesn't depend on anything else. It lives deep inside of you—the small drop of universe energy. Your soul connects to the vast beautiful energy of the universe.

Is it possible to be completely connected to your soul and therefore feel the universe's happiness all the time? Yes, it is called *enlightenment*! From my personal experience, only a very small percentage of people are on a path of personal development and growth. Fewer still achieve total and complete enlightenment. But even glimpses of this feeling, this happiness, is a billion times (yes, with a B) more significant than the artificial happiness felt within the average social conventions and routines.

Several years ago, I was hiking in a beautiful part of Spain, in the region of Extremadura. While hiking, I stumbled on a huge meadow next to stunning mountains. It was a beautiful spring day, not too hot and not too cold. The sky was clear blue. The meadow was enormous in size, with several trees scattered in the midst of it. While the meadow could have accommodated thousands of sheep, I could only see twenty. All twenty were congregated in a two-meter-squared spot. They had acres of fresh grass to eat and walk on but were on top of each other in a patch of beaten down, dirty grass. Why? Because it was their comfort zone.

The sheep were willing to forfeit the benefits of the meadow for the feeling of safety.

If the sheep would just lift their heads and look around, they would see they are in the middle of an amazing and unbelievably beautiful place. They would notice the vast amount of green grass for them to enjoy in the meadow around them, the blue mountains, and the bright sun in the blue sky. Similarly, if we shift our perspectives, we could see the amazing opportunities and endless possibilities around us. We will see past our patches of beaten down, dirty grass.

Unfortunately, this is how most people live their whole lives—like the sheep in the meadow. While the sheep might not have a choice due to their limited mental capacity to see the big picture or understand personal happiness, you do! If you are willing to lift your head and look around for opportunities that would make you happy, you can live an unbelievable life. I call this process *re-programing.* Re-program in a way that allows you to structure your life to achieve happiness.

Unfortunately, most people will live their whole lives without awakening to their inner energy. They might be successful people in society; they might not be successful people in society. The common theme is that most will not get to feel their connection with the universe and therefore will never feel the deep happiness of that connection—the same connection they felt so naturally when they came into this world, and the same connection they felt intuitively and effortlessly when they were kids. The same connection that still lives deep inside, covered by layers and layers of social programming to follow social convention, blocking the universe's energy.

Luckily, in some cases, intuition sends a small ray of light from under all the layers of programming, allowing the person to notice that something is missing in their life structure. The person might not know what is wrong, but there is a feeling that something is missing. Since there are many layers covering this person's natural intuition, the rays felt are very small. Nevertheless, there is a feeling that something is missing from life, even if the person is very successful in society.

Most people, when they get these small glimpses of intuitive energy, will just ignore it, as it's unfamiliar and not something they have been taught to notice. But others instinctively feel there is something there, an internal feeling that something is missing, pulling them somewhere, even if the pull is very faint. This instinctive openness to small glimpses of our internal energy or light, despite being covered by endless layers of social programming, is a guiding light for us to find the happiness engraved in our central processing units (CPUs). If you are reading this book, it means that you have experienced this sensation. This process of peeling away layers of social programming and slowly connecting to more and more of the universe's energy has many names and billions of pages written on it. I consider it personal growth, and the process of connecting with my inner light.

Personal growth can happen in endless ways. It can take the shape of a religious path, spiritual path, mindset change, or the combination of all three. But the common and most important theme is that it is a process of digging through all the layers of external programming to discover and connect to one's soul—and through it, to the universe's energy, which, at its core, is what will allow you to feel pure happiness and pure love. Nothing in the physical world can come close to the limitlessness magnitude of this energy, and the amazing fact is that the connection interface to this unlimited and indescribable bliss is already imprinted in you. All you need to do is to uncover it within yourself...

If you are reading this book, I suspect you are aware of this energy inside of you. Maybe you feel small glimpses of it deep inside of you, penetrating through the many layers of social programming. Perhaps you are already on a personal path of growth and personal development. If you are on any stage of this path and journey to find your happiness and live the best life you can, whether in the beginning or advanced, I hope that this book can help and guide you on this amazing journey.

# PART II: UNDERSTANDING YOURSELF AND THE UNIVERSE'S ENERGY

# THE EGO AND THE MIND

In the development of humankind, through thousands of years of creating social structures that enable human beings to function in societies, people created endless layers of social programming. As discussed before, the purpose of social programming is to create social cohesion and allow society to function. So, what is the problem? The social programming we have adopted is not designed to connect us with our souls. The structures that are socially programmed in us are focused only on the functioning of the society, and are based on ego.

The ego is our mind-based concept of ourselves. Most people see themselves and identify themselves as their ego. In most modern societies, ego is a creation of the socially programmed mind. We are programmed from birth to follow a very specific path in life, and that path is based on the socially programmed identity of our ego. The ego, if we view it as an 'entity', is not connected to the energy of the universe. Ego focuses only on the physical: what we want and desire but does not focus and does not know how to find our inner happiness. And so almost all of us are chasing our wants and desires, but neglect to search and find our happiness. In the current basic human condition, we are controlled by our egos. Our ego controls our minds and thoughts, which in turn controls our bodies and actions.

In theory, if we want to find our happiness, we should identify as the entity inside of us that focuses on our happiness and harmony- our soul, as opposed to identifying with the entity inside of us that focuses on our desires- our ego. Our souls should help us to chart our paths to our happiness. Our brains and minds direct our day-to-day physical activities we need and want to perform, like eating, grooming, sleeping, working, etc. While our souls, which are in constant contact with the energy of the universe, should show us the ways to create harmony and happiness in our lives. This should allow us to achieve physical goals in conjunction to achieving happiness and harmony. Unfortunately, this isn't how most people structure and live their lives.

To understand it in the most simplistic way, I separate our identity into three parts. All three exist inside of us.

1. Our mind
2. Our ego (controlling entity of the control center, the mind)
3. Our soul (can also be controlling entity of control center)

Our mind and brain can be viewed as our control center. All the activities we are performing and everything we are doing, thinking and planning goes through the control center. This is our operational center. The question is who is in charge of the control center? There are only two options, it's either our ego or our soul.

The socially programmed ego is small, nonproductive, full of desires and wants and lacks happiness. The ego wants to ensure the survival of ego itself.

The soul is large, it is connected to the infinite energy and the wisdom of the universe. The soul is focused on finding harmony and balance in everything, and by doing so can show us the path to our happiness.

Most of the people live their lives under the control of their egos. When someone is unaware an *egoistic* entity controls their actions, they live in a potentially chaotic routine without the possibility of reaching happiness. From the ego's standpoint, this is good, as it continuously sends fear and anxiety signals to keep the body and mind distracted so it can continue its control over the entity (the human) and therefore assure its (the ego) survival. The result is ongoing anxiety and unhappiness.

Since the ego is completely self-focused, it will always try to stay in full control. It will not allow any competition. It blocks the connection between the mind and soul. Egos know that if we connect to our souls and feel the amazing bliss provided by the universe's energy, we will not want to live under its control. As long as we are in a constant state of distress—our minds and bodies busy with the distressing, distracting thoughts our egos generate—ego is able to stay in control of us.

Many spiritual leaders dedicate a lot of their teachings to dealing with ego and eliminating ego. They teach us that our egos block our connections to the energy of the universe. They also teach that when energy is blocked, our productivity and success in the physical world diminishes, we cannot feel internal happiness, and our quality of life suffers. This type of existence will, in turn, result in disharmony and suffering, regardless of whether we have achieved success based on social standards.

What happens when we don't allow egos to take over our bodies, minds, and actions? What happens when we control our egos? We *feel* the connections to our souls. We notice the blissful glimpses of harmony and happiness that come from connecting to, and feeling, the energy of the universe inside and around us. If we can fully control our egos and fully live through the connection to our souls, we become enlightened.

How do you control your ego? As always, the first step is to understand the issue. Once you understand your ego is the source of your suffering, you can figure out what to do about it. Evaluate your actions and the circular thought cycles in your mind. Notice how a lot of your anxiety, anger, frustration, etc., comes from negative thought loops that are constantly circulating in your head. Who or what is generating these thought loops? While it's true that your mind is generating these thoughts, remember your mind is the *control centre*, not the *controller*. The mind is a tool, an amazing tool, that acts as a super sophisticated control centre for the body. If you look carefully, you might discover that your ego might be the controller of the control centre.

Once you understand these concepts, you'll see your ego in action. You will see your ego acting up in various situations. You'll notice your ego generating circular thoughts that trigger negative emotions like fear, anxiety, anger, frustration, and discomfort. Your ego has a lot of power over how you see your world . . until you take action. When you let your soul guide you and be in charge, happiness, harmony and balance will enter your life.

# CONSCIOUSNESS

Everyone is aware of their body and mind, but most people are not aware of their consciousness. There are many definitions for consciousness, but for the purpose of the discussions in this book, I define consciousness as the universe's energy that exists in each of us. Our souls are a small drop of the universe's energy inside of us, and therefore are part of the universe's consciousness.

In most people, their consciousness is hidden deep inside their bodies. They are not aware of the presence of this energy, and therefore have no connection with it. Their minds control their actions, and as we have discussed in the previous chapter, their minds are controlled by their egos.

What is the alternative?

To reach happiness, we need to operate from our consciousness. In order to do that, we need to understand how consciousness works.

The universe consists of energy. A small part of this energy is visible to us. We see and sense the energy in our physical world. The physical world happens to be the coarsest type of energy there is. But in reality, this is only a tiny part of the energy that exists in the universe. The higher planes (of energy) which we can't sense with our five senses, consist of a much finer energy. Although we can't see it, this finer energy is harmonious and beautiful. The universe consists of many planes with different types of energy—our physical world being the lowest in quality and harmony. There are various higher planes, which are full of pure, beautiful, and harmonious energy.

The little drop of energy that sits inside each human is part of a much larger consciousness, that is to say it is a part of a much larger energy universe. Each of us has a much larger consciousness that is connected to the consciousness of the universe. The rest of our vast consciousness exists as energy in other energetic planes. In order to reach our deep inner happiness, we need to connect our little drop of consciousness with our big consciousness- the universe's energy.

What is stopping us from doing that? Our egos. Remember, the ego wants to stay in control.

Once we open the channel, so our little consciousness connects with our big consciousness on a higher plane, the energy of the entire universe opens to us. When this happens, we feel the universe's energy flowing into our physical body as it shines through us. This is the state of full harmony and internal happiness.

When this state is achieved, the difficulties of the physical world do not bother us—we feel the pure energy of the universe instead. A full connection between our souls, higher consciousness, and the energy of the universe is *enlightenment*, and it could take a long time to achieve. Every step we take in our own self-development and growth process, opens that connection further. Every step closer exposes us to the light and the blessings of the universe's energy. This is like hiking a beautiful mountain. Although the trek is physically difficult, every new height reached reveals a more beautiful view. Every step made in the self-development process exposes a better perspective of ourselves and allows more beautiful energy to flow into our bodies and lives.

When enlightenment is reached, our physical existence is created by our consciousness, our soul, and the consciousness of the universe—not the ego. We can operate our daily routines while staying connected to our higher consciousness. We can experience constant awareness of its presence, and work to keep the energy flowing. Developing the energy flow between a higher and lower consciousness, which is our self-development and growth, can be done through various methods discussed later in this book, including meditation.

Our consciousness can go up and down within the various planes. When it is down, it's in our physical body. When it's connected with the consciousness of the universe, the activities we do in the physical world will be done with the intelligence, blessing, and happiness of the universe. When we are able to maintain the connection with our higher consciousness, our actions in the physical world will be at a higher level and higher intelligence because we will govern ourselves not just by our egos but also by the intelligence of the universe. Every action we take in the physical world will have the essence of the universe's energy in it, and when our actions are influenced by the flow of the universe's energy, successful outcomes are much more probable. This basically means that if we connect to our higher consciousness, not only will we be more successful at what we are trying to achieve in the physical world, but we will also find our internal happiness.

More importantly, operating in that kind of state will enable harmony. And living in harmony results in internal happiness.

On the other hand, if we allow our egos to control our decisions and our minds, then we are using only the physical intelligence of our body and completely ignoring a much more powerful tool with a much higher intelligence. Furthermore, this little brain, our ego as it's called in some eastern philosophies, can't lead us to any extraordinary achievements in the physical world. Nor can it help us find internal happiness and harmony. Great things in the physical world usually require the universe, its wisdom and energy, and its 'big brain'. The ego-controlled mind is often just not strong enough to create great things in any aspect of our lives. More importantly, life in the physical world will always be in a state of unhappiness and dissatisfaction because that's how ego works. Ego's modus operandi is to be in a constant state of unhappiness and dissatisfaction.

Once we open the channel of communication with our internal consciousness, our soul will find a clear path to go up and down between our physical bodies on earth and our higher consciousness on the energetic planes. When we do that, our consciousness will be connected with the consciousness of the universe, allowing us to be in our physical body and the consciousness of the universe simultaneously. The universe's energy flow will enhance and improve the performance of our physical bodies in the physical world and allow us to thrive in a state of presence, happiness, and consciousness.

Once you embark on this personal development process, you will see glimpses of internal happiness. These glimpses of internal happiness will signal that you are on the right path. You will feel some sort of internal satisfaction and connection, which is your intuition communicating your progress in the right direction. This type of satisfaction will feel different from the satisfaction of getting a new gadget. It will be a much deeper, more profound feeling of harmony, and will remain with you as long as you continue to self-develop and stay connected to the energy of the universe. Operating your life from your higher consciousness, as opposed to your ego, can help you find your internal harmony and happiness, but it can also help you accomplish a much higher level of success in the physical world.

How does being connected to the universe's energy get you on the path to happiness? By connecting to the universe's energy, you have access to a higher *quality* of energy. During day-to-day routines, you are normally operating on a lower quality energy that is mainly generated by your ego and the egos of the people surrounding you. This lower quality energy is the normal, accepted state of mind for most people, and most day-to-day routines are built on this lower energy quality. This lower quality energy is not harmonious because almost everybody is under their ego's control. This type of energy is focused on the desires for *more*—the most extreme example being wars between nations, which often stem from the people's collective egos wanting more of something, like natural resources, land, influence, etc. This same low energy exists in various acts of crimes, committed by people who desire something and use force to get it. It can also be seen in negative workplace scenarios, as well as arguments between friends and partners. In all these situations, higher energy is not present, creating chaos versus harmony.

When you connect to your higher consciousness on a higher plane, and are not operating from your ego, you discover a completely different quality of energy—a higher quality of energy. This energy is the pure energy of the universe. Bringing this energy into your day-to-day physical life creates harmony. This harmony, in turn, brings you peace, which makes you happy. This type of happiness is much more profound than any superficial happiness derived from purchasing something you desire. This type of happiness depends totally on you, not on other people or situations to achieve it. And this type of happiness doesn't fade with time.

If you're still not sure why it's vital to connect with your soul, control your ego, or listen to your intuition, don't worry, there is more to come. Keep reading.

# INTUITION

Most people tend to rely on their brain's logic as the main tool for making short and long-term decisions. From basic daily small choices to career decisions and selecting life partners. Society is built on the concept that logic-based decision-making is the only way (and the best way) to go through life. From kindergarten through university, this process is constantly and repeatedly enforced and programmed into us. We are taught there is only one way to make decisions: the methodical process of analysis.

Of course, people make impulsive decisions based on impulse emotions like fear and desire, which of course never leads to a good decisions. Therefore, it makes sense that we are taught that decisions are *successful* or *good* when they are made through careful, well-thought out, logic-based rationale. We apply this process not only to work-related issues, financial choices, or purchases, but also to choosing our partners. We make pro and con lists to choose our vacations, our career paths, our life partners, and whether to get married.

It's fair to say logic is an amazing tool. Our brains contain billions of cells that enable us to do tremendous amounts of calculations to help us with decision-making. The problem is that our brains are not the only tool at our disposal and might not be the best tool to maximize happiness. If we want to reach our full potential in life, we need to improve and enhance our decision-making.

How? What other tools do we have?

The answer is intuition!

What is intuition? Intuition is the communication between the universe's energy and our souls—which is, if you've forgotten, a small drop of the universe's energy that resides inside every living being. Intuition is the messenger system from your soul to your brain, and it comes through as emotions and feelings. Some people refer to this communication as a *gut feeling*, as if something in the *gut* is pushing you to pursue an action or make a certain decision.

Many people believe that intuition is the same as instinct, but this is, in fact, incorrect. So, the first step in understanding intuition is to distinguish it from instinct. Instinct is encoded in our DNA and is used by our bodies to react to different situations. For example, a lion's DNA tells him that he is a hunter, and deer are his prey. He knows that this is what allows him to nourish himself and therefore survive, so the lion will rely on his instinct and follow his DNA-encoded survival guide without questioning it. It is something he simply knows. Female turtles go to the beach where they were born, at a specific time, and in specific weather conditions, to lay their eggs. It is not something to be challenged or analysed; they simply know what they need to do because it's part of their DNA, their imprinted instincts. Salmon knows they must spawn in the same river in which they were hatched, so they follow their instincts and swim upstream against the current, jump over waterfalls, and battle bears and other predators to reach the shallow waters of their ancestors. In humans, our flight or fight instincts kick in when faced with danger. None of these actions happen after making lists of pros and cons, and none are debated. Instinct is embedded in our DNA. It is designed to help us survive.

As important as instincts are for survival, they are not designed to help us maximize our potential in life, and they definitely don't lead to happiness. For that, we have our intuition...

Sadly, people rarely rely on their intuition. Most people never learn how to use it or incorporate it into the decision-making process. Here we need to understand how we are designed. Every human has a body, which is a complex, highly organized structure of cells that work together to sustain life. No matter the shape, race, sex, or size of the body, we can only marvel at the magnificence of trillions of individual cells working together in perfect harmony to accomplish the miracle of physical life. The brain is the control centre, where our conscious and unconscious tasks are directed and supervised. Our brains guide us through tasks—from day-to-day chores, to accomplishing huge scientific feats. Indeed, the brain is a powerful tool at our disposal, but we shouldn't underestimate the power of our souls.

As mentioned before, your soul is formed of the universe's energy. Whether you call it divine energy, God's energy, or the universe's energy, in the end, this energy remains the same and it exists inside every living being on earth. The soul is what differentiates a dead body from a living one. Souls do not inhabit dead bodies.

Most people are not aware of this energy and are certainly not in contact with their own drop of the divine. This is because our social system does not teach about souls. We are taught, throughout our education and beyond, that we have a body and a brain, but we are not taught that we contain divine energy or how to connect to it.

Remember, the energy inside us is the same energy as the universe's energy, which means that if we connect our brains to our little drop of the universe's energy, we will have access to the knowledge and wisdom of the universe. It goes without saying that the universe has much more significant knowledge and wisdom than all our human knowledge combined—multiplied by trillions. Because the wisdom of the universe is trillions of times greater than we are, using it would allow us to tap into a much more powerful and vastly larger wisdom and knowledge base than simply relying on our brain and logic.

So, how do we connect our internal energy, our souls, with the energy of the universe? *Through intuition.* Our intuition is the interface between the universe and us. The communication is done by our souls sending us guidance and direction through internal feelings.

The most successful people in any area of life, whether it's business, the arts, politics, sports, entertainment, etc., are people who connect to and are guided by their intuition and combine it with their logic and physical skills. The stronger the connection, the more successful the person is. These people reach their full potential. Those who do not, are less successful.

Intuition opens the possibility of connection with a higher level of wisdom. It has access to the wisdom of the universe, a wisdom beyond the limits of human logic. In order to achieve above-average results, you must tap into above-average knowledge and exceptional decision-making skills. Your mental capacity, bright as you may be, simply does not have the ability to allow that. The universe's knowledge is accessible to you exclusively through your soul, and your intuition is the medium used to process it.

When you learn to listen to your intuition, you can use it in all of life's aspects: professionally, personally, creatively, and beyond. Whatever you choose to accomplish, whether it be financial success, spiritual development, or social goals, you've got tools at your disposal. When facing any decision or goal, you can use your intuition together with your brain's logic to achieve great results. In spiritual writings, the human brain is often referred to as *the little brain*. When we are connected to the universe's energy and wisdom, resulting in intuitive guidance, this is known as *the big brain*.

Just imagine the scale of possibilities. The average Western education does not expose you to the knowledge of the universe wisdom and energy. Yet, you can become a beneficiary of this knowledge and reach your full potential when you tap into the limitlessly rich knowledge available through your intuition.

How do you develop and establish this communication?

The key is to distinguish your intuition from the background noise of your brain. Your mind generates a large amount of background thoughts, most of which are a useless continuous loop of things that happened to you, bother you, and your fears and desires. These thoughts offer no value—they just keep on circulating in your head. They also consume a lot of energy and block your intuition by masking it with a constant stream of fog or *thought noise*. Understand your intuition is there, built into you, and all you need to do is be attentive and learn to distinguish it from the habitual noise of the mind. Become sensitive to the recognition of these feelings.

In the beginning, it may feel very vague, and you may not know if it's a frivolous thought or your intuition giving directions. To develop the ability to differentiate the two, simply use trial and error. You might feel a certain gut feeling telling you to pursue something. You might follow the path led by this emotion. Where you end up will tell you which of the two it was. If you follow your intuition, it will lead you to a better place. If you mistakenly follow one of your brain's noise thoughts, your situation will not improve. When you feel good, like you've made a positive improvement, this place will feel right, and you'll know you've followed your intuition's guidance. If your decisions led you to a path that doesn't feel right, you've followed your brain's thought noise. In both cases, note what kind of feeling you followed and try to distinguish it. This learning will help you follow the universe's communication next time you have to make a decision.

First, it's better to practice this on insignificant, daily decisions. For example, if you are thinking of going on a vacation and can't decide which one to do, see if you can listen to your intuition to help you pick the one that feels better. Or, if you are looking to choose a personal trainer, and they all seem qualified, use your intuition to choose the right trainer for you. Or, you might be trying to figure out what to do next weekend. Try to use your intuition to guide you to the activity that is calling you the most. As you get better in identifying your intuition, you can start using it for more and more significant decisions. The amazing thing is that you can use your intuition for decision making in all areas of your life, like your career, relationships, partnerships, businesses, spiritual development, etc. It's important to remember that your intuition gives you the general best direction, like a good life compass, but once you have the direction, it's important to use it in conjunction with your brain's logic to figure out the best path in that direction. This way, you use all your tools to achieve goals, self-reflect, grow, and improve your life.

As you learn how to use your intuition with small decisions, try combinations of your old ways of decision making, like making pro and con lists. You can also ask your intuition questions and see what it comes up with. You then take time to ponder the decision, continually asking yourself the same question without relying on your brain to analyse it and answer. Pay attention to how you feel. At some point, you may find you experience a sensation that gives you a small nudge towards a course of action. It is almost like the beginning or precursor to a developed thought. It is a sensation that later turns into a thought. It is nothing more than a possibility.

You might not know if it's your intuition guiding you, but if you follow the guidance and find it works out well, the positive results are probably because the universe was open to you when you accessed it. Try another decision, maybe a slightly larger one, and again ponder it, running this same process. Let the question float within you until you receive another small sensation. Then, follow suit.

Slowly but surely, these sensations will become clearer and louder, and recognizing them will no longer be difficult. That is the communication device between you and the universe improving through exercise. Like anything else in the physical world, what is exercised and practiced is improved. It is simply exercising the muscles of intuition. The more it is used, the more you can tap into it, and the more useful it will become. There is no end because the knowledge of the universe is, in fact, endless, so learning to embrace and strengthen your ability to tap into the universe's energy and knowledge will present new possibilities in your life.

# VIBRATION

Every object in the world has a *vibration*. Every object vibrates on a different vibration frequency. We as humans are mostly unaware of this fact and therefore ignore it. But we feel these frequencies in many indirect ways. For instance, when you look at a beautiful flower, you see the physical beauty of it while unconsciously feeling the beautiful vibration of that flower. Or the opposite example: when you enter a room or place and immediately feel uncomfortable. You don't know why you experience that feeling, but you feel the vibration frequency of the people in the room, and that vibration frequency makes you uncomfortable because it's not compatible with your vibration frequency. The same can be said when you meet a new person you are immediately drawn to. You might be drawn to physical attributes or the personality of that person, but many times it's the underlying vibration of that person that feels comfortable and attracts you.

Why is all this relevant?

You are looking to find your happiness. To find your happiness, you need to find your balance. To find your balance, you need to align your internal vibration frequency to the harmonious frequency of the universe.

The problem with connecting to the universe's energy is that the vibration of the average human body living in a city in the modern world is completely disconnected from to the vibration of the universe. We are used to living in societies that have completely different vibrations than the natural vibration of the universe. Most people live in big, congested, and crowded cities. They are surrounded by aggressive traffic, anxious people, various levels of crime and suffering, fast modern life, constant news and information flow, social media, etc. All of these have completely different vibrations than the universe. Furthermore, the modern world works in such a way that we are constantly bombarded by information. Most of the information is random but more importantly a lot of this information is negative and therefore has a negative vibration frequency, whether we are aware of it or not. This makes our bodies vibrate in the same or similar vibration as the constant noise that surrounds us. This vibration is very quick and shallow. This is the vibrational frequency of a busy material world.

We are bombarded by nonstop information, which is mostly meaningless, and mostly detrimental to our quality of life. The problem is not the information itself, but the vibration of this information.

If you take a moment to notice the news, you will discover the vast majority is a list of negative events that transpired in your area over the last twenty-four hours. If there weren't enough negative events in your area, the negative events from other areas of the world are presented, even when they have no relevance to you. So, not only are you bombarded by endless streams of information, but the stream of information is mostly negative and not relevant to your life. Media networks will count how many people have been murdered or subjected to various types of violence in the last twenty-four hours. They'll tell you how many car accidents occurred, how many fires happened, how many burglaries took place, and how many people died from diseases. Networks will talk about the same issues in other parts of the world, even when most people listening to the news can't spot these places on a map. Now add the constant stream of gossip you receive from social media, your friends, relatives, partners, etc., and you will see your life is filled to the brim with negative vibrations.

Everybody around you is exposed to the same vibration, so they vibrate on the same negative vibrational frequency that surrounds you, which is completely different from the frequency of the universe. Because this vibration frequency is mostly negative and does not correspond to the harmonious vibrational frequency of the universe, most people feel anxious, restless, discomfort, fearful, etc. This is why experiencing nature feels very different. Surrounded by nature, the body relaxes. In nature, you feel the vibration of the universe and your body starts moving from the hectic, unsettled, negative vibrations of the city and society to the positive, calming, peaceful, and natural vibration of the universe. Nature is designed that way. Even if this feeling is not conscious, it is always there. That's why people go hiking and spend time in nature, parks, or beaches.

Now that you understand that negative vibrations surround you, what can be done about it?

To connect to your soul and find happiness, you need to fix your vibrational frequency. Which means that you need to align your body's vibration to the vibration of the universe.

There are several ways to improve your vibrational frequency. While some of the negative vibrations around you are absorbed by your body, most are taken in through your mind. The first step is always awareness. By being aware of the information and the vibration quality of this information flow you are subjecting yourself to and absorbing during your day-to-day life, you can be more aware of the quality of energy that enters your mind. For example, if you are listening and watching news all days long and they are constantly transmitting negative vibration frequency, you need to be aware of it. Just by being aware, you will reduce the negative effects of it. By being aware of the quality of the vibration you are exposing yourself to, you might decide to moderate or reduce the intake of this type of information and the negative vibration it transmits.

The second step is to find and build positive energy surroundings for your body to absorb and align with the frequency and energy of the universe. This means that you can create a surrounding for yourself that is calm and nurturing, or at least spend some of your time in that type of environment. How do you know if you are in that type of positive environment? If you feel calm and at ease, then you are. If you feel anxious and uncomfortable, you aren't. It would be beneficial to spend at least part of your day in an environment that gives you positive energy and vibration. Since your body absorbs the vibrational frequencies surrounding it, the simplest way to align with the vibrational frequency of the universe is to spend time in nature. More on this in a separate chapter.

Many spiritual teachings talk about being *present, in the here,* and, *in the now*. Our minds, instead of being jumpy, shallow, or fast, need to become stable and quiet to connect and align with the calm vibration of the universe. This is very hard to do because the mind constantly resists. The mind is used to operating on a super-fast frequency, the same super-fast frequency it is constantly bombarded with.

One way to calm your mind is meditation. The purpose of meditation is to calm the mind and move it closer to the universe's vibration. There are many meditation techniques, and different people will connect using different techniques. The common theme is to disconnect the mind from the constant thought routine that is enhanced and multiplied by our modern world and to bring it to a state of calm, and beautiful vibrational frequency—the vibrational frequency of the universe. I will elaborate on meditation in a separate chapter.

# PAINBODY

*Painbody* is something that accumulates in you over many years of reacting the same way to situations that affect you negatively, annoy you, and trigger you. It's a buildup of negative pain energy. Ekhart Tolle in his books calls it Painbody—which I believe describes it well. Ekhart Tolle talks about Painbody in detail and in extremely useful ways in his various writings, and my goal here is to expand on his teachings from my standpoint, experience, and understanding.

Throughout your life, when you feel psychological pain and suffering in different situations, you are affected negatively. Maybe you didn't like a specific situation or event and now feel negativity towards it. Every time you react with a negative emotion to such a situation, this negative energy stays inside of you and keeps accumulating over time, often becoming a very large and dense negative energy build up. This negative energy build up inside of you – Painbody - can be accumulated and grow during your whole life time. We might even bring Painbody from previous lives. Every time a new but similar negative situation occurs in your day-to-day life, you think that you are responding to that current occurrence, but in reality, it immediately triggers your Painbody. When that happens, your Painbody awakens and takes over your response. Suddenly you find yourself responding in a much more significant way to even a small occurrence. You don't understand why this has happened and why you have overreacted to a relatively small occurrence. In reality, it wasn't you, your Painbody took psychological control over you. The overreaction was because of the Painbody reacting based on past experiences and all of the associated accumulated negative energy. The time that the Painbody will stay in control depends on the size of the Painbody, eventually it will subside again into our subconscious and relinquish control over us. This Painbody inside us can be stagnant until it's triggered the next time, and we might not be aware it even exists. Yet it will come to life immediately and take over when it's triggered by a negative event again and again, creating emotions such as rage, anger, impatience, sadness, fear, or anxiety. When triggered, Painbody takes over and you act and behave under the influence of Painbody until it rescinds into the depths of your psychology, awaiting the next trigger event.

Each time Painbody is awakened, it grows stronger and generates a larger negative response. When triggered, you don't only respond to that specific situation, you respond to the millions or billions of similar situations you have experienced over your lifetime, especially if you have reacted the same way and felt the same negative feelings. Your response can be completely disproportional to what is happening because you are responding to an accumulation of negative feelings from the past. Not only do you go through life carrying these accumulated negative feelings towards certain situations, but you also have multiple Painbodies, and several can be triggered at any point. You might notice these when you respond negatively during a minor event that would have otherwise made you only slightly upset or not affected you at all.

Painbody keeps growing and growing . . . until you do something about it.

The first and most important step is to be aware you have Painbodies inside you. The moment you understand what is happening to you, and you can see your Painbody jumping on you and taking control over you, you can stop it. Even if you can't stop the negative feelings inside of you, you can limit Painbody's power. The process would work as follows:

1. You are suddenly triggered by something, and you start feeling negative emotions. You might feel upset, angry, fearful, uncomfortable, or any other negative feeling.

2. Take a minute to notice what is happening to you (inside of you). Ask yourself, *where are these negative feelings coming from?* Think about the source of these negative feelings, the Painbody is activated.

3. Each time you experience a negative feeling, notice how Painbody was awakened and triggered, and your reaction to it. You will get closer to dealing with the source of the problem.

In the beginning, the negative feelings will not go away. Because Painbody is so ingrained in you, and it is so dense, it will not dissipate by just noticing it. The denser the Painbody is, the longer the process of clearing that Painbody will be. For example, a not very dense Painbody might be completely eliminated just by noticing it inside of you. Denser Painbodies that have been living inside of you for a long time and have been accumulating their negative energy for years or even decades, will require much more work to clear out. But in all cases, to achieve happiness, you need to deal with and clear the Painbodies that live inside you.

By noticing and looking at Painbody while it flares up inside of you, two things will happen. First, the negative reaction connected to that Painbody will be at a lower level. Meaning, just by watching and noticing, the level of pain you feel from the flare up will be reduced. You still can't stop Painbody taking over, but the level of control that Painbody has over you will be lowered, and the pain you will feel will be lower as well. You will still be upset, uncomfortable, fearful, in pain, angry, etc., but on a lower level. You will also know that the negative emotions you are feeling are due to some triggered negative energy inside of you, not the situation itself. This is the beginning of freeing yourself from the Painbody.

The moment you know Painbody has been triggered, you also know it's a foreign entity in control of you. By noticing this and being aware of it you are shining the light of consciousness on it. And so, the moment you shine the light of your consciousness on this foreign entity inside of you, the density of it will be reduced. Eckhart Tolle, in his books, aptly writes that "Everything that is exposed to light becomes light itself." As time goes by, and you continue watching it, you will notice Painbody sooner. The sooner you notice this happening, the lower the level of control and pain the Painbody generates. If, in the beginning, you were in a turmoil of emotions when triggered, then several hours later you understood that it was the Painbody triggered. As you do this more and more, you will see Painbody much sooner. The earlier you notice the triggering of Painbody in you, the less intense the negative emotions and duration. When you notice the Painbody in real time, you will automatically take away some level of control it has over you.

The more you understand the source of your negative emotions, the fewer *new* Painbodies will be created. Furthermore, if you are unconscious of your Painbodies getting triggered, each time a Painbody will get triggered it will grow and add more negative energy to itself. It will be easier to trigger it the next time and the level of negative emotions will be higher. But if you are aware of what is going on inside of you, while it is happening or afterwards, you can prevent the Painbody from growing and intensifying. On the contrary, you will take energy away from it and therefore decrease it over time.

It is important to know that you are not able to get rid of Painbody right away, just by understanding the process. Painbodies entrench themselves in us for many years and thousands of similar reactions to similar situations. But it's important to know that you can get rid of the Painbodies over time, by doing the work, and putting the effort into it.

The way you get rid of Painbody is by continuously noticing when you are triggered and not letting the Painbody take over. This will take the power away from Painbody and will re-program your mind's muscle memory to not react negatively to previously triggering events. Each time you do that, the negative energy of the Painbody will not be able to grow, and the ability of the Painbody to control you will disappear. You will eventually have the ability see the Painbody's attempts to take over even before it happens. Then, you can send love and positive energy to it to eliminate its negative power in real time.

At the end of the day, if you are able to clean the accumulated negative energy inside of you (your Painbodies) you will live a much freer life. You will not be affected by negative situations and day-to-day circumstances that used to trigger you. The implication of this is profound. You'll be free to live your life in a positive state of mind. In essence, by getting rid of the

Painbodies, you take back control of yourself. You will not be triggered and dragged into profound negative emotions by situations that used to do so on a daily basis. The less negative emotional episodes you are experiencing in your life, the more positive and happier your life will be.

# KARMA

To start with, it's important to note that karma comes from Eastern philosophical and religious teachings like Buddhism. These teachings are vast and deep, so I will not go into the traditional teachings of karma, and instead try to explain my basic understanding of it.

We are born into this world with a little drop of the universe's energy inside of us- our soul. This drop of energy is part of a big ocean of energy, which is the energy of the universe. Energy never dies—just transforms. Energy cannot be destroyed. Energy can only shift forms. So, where does this little drop of universe energy come from before we are born into the physical world?

My understanding is that this little drop of universe energy, our soul, comes from a different plane of existence. We experience physical life in the physical plane (physical world), and most of the people in Western societies believe this is the only plane. In the physical plane, we pursue physical goals and are not aware of any other energetic planes because they are not taught through social programming—even though there is endless amounts of information and millions of books written on this topic. Most people ignore it because it is not part of what society considers mainstream understanding. Therefore, as we have discussed before, it is not taught in schools.

Remember, society is focused on the direction that will make society work. For society, it's important that people stay stable, pay their taxes, go to work, raise their kids, and take care of their families. Society never focuses on personal growth or personal happiness because these are not important for society. Happiness doesn't pay taxes. People in society feel, as they are programmed to think, that there is one plane and that is the physical plane. In this one plane, our life takes place.

As we have discussed before, inside of each and every one of us there exists a drop of the universe's energy. When we are born in the physical world, what is born is the physical body, which is unique every time. Our bodies and personalities are based on our parent's DNA, but what is not created by our parents, is our soul. This is the drop of energy that comes into the body when the baby develops enough to be a human before birth. That soul enters the body and merges with it. Our soul has chosen to be born to a specific set of parents and a specific set of circumstances, because of the lessons it needs to learn in this life. The combination of the physical form and the energy of the soul makes a human being.

That energy comes from a different plane. The energy could have been reincarnated many times before into other bodies. It will keep on reincarnating until it accomplishes the goals it needs to accomplish, which I will talk about later in this chapter.

When two humans, a man and woman, create a baby, a new body starts to form. When the brain forms, the soul enters the body, creating a full package. Every human being has a drop of the universe's energy in them. Everybody is born with a soul. What is the purpose of this energy? What is the purpose of the soul, and why does it reincarnate? Why are we here in the physical world?

My understanding is that this drop of universe energy wants to reunite with the universe's big ocean of energy. The universe's ocean of energy exists in a constant state of harmony and peace and spans across all planes of existence. The little drop of energy inside of us wants to reunite with the harmonious ocean of the universe's energy. As we all know, life on the physical plane is not harmonious nor peaceful. It is full of conflict and drama. It is designed to be that way. In order to reunite with the ocean of universe energy the soul needs to grow through experiencing certain lessons in the physical world. Self-growth and self-development are the process of listening to our soul telling us what lessons it needs to learn and what blocks it needs to overcome, by aligning our life with the energy of the universe. This process of our souls growing, advancing and learning life lessons through physical life experiences during each reincarnation is an important part of *Karma*. By establishing the connection with our inner energy, our souls, and therefore with the universe's energy, not only do we find the harmony and inner peace we seek, but we also are able to understand our soul's life lessons. On this path of personal growth, we not only develop as people and become better versions of ourselves, but we also advance our souls development as well as bring the universe's harmony and peace to our physical lives.

The lives most people live on the physical plane does not reflect what our soul's want and need to accomplish. The only exception to this is people on a path of self-development and growth. This group of people figured out through listening to their intuition and the discovery of their inner self, that they can, and need, to be connected with their souls. Once people realize this energy, several things happen. One, a sense of harmony and peace enters their lives. The stronger the connection, the stronger the sense of harmony and peace. Two, they know their soul needs to develop and grow, which is the process of self-growth and development. The more that growth and self-development happens, the more energy the person has in the physical world.

Once a person establishes a connection with their inner energy, that person starts to feel the bliss of this connection in their day-to-day life. The next step in self-development is to figure out what specific development issues their soul needs and wants to accomplish in this life cycle. I will elaborate on this later, but for now, we need to know that every soul has different needs and issues it brings from previous lives, previous reincarnations, which is *Karma.* These issues and goals need to be developed and resolved on the physical plane. This is why we are born into a specific set of circumstances, like a specific family, country, or socioeconomic situation. Our soul chooses a specific set of circumstances so it can develop and learn through the experience.

Before entering the body of a foetus, the soul chooses the life circumstances it believes will be best for it to learn the lessons it needs and face the issues it needs to overcome.

Why does the soul come from a higher plane (non-physical plane) to the lower physical plane (physical world)?

Because the physical plane is the only place where the soul can learn and grow. In essence, the physical plane is a school for the soul to learn how to overcome the issues holding it back from reaching a higher energetic level. Once the soul has grown enough, through many reincarnations, it does not need to reincarnate into the physical world.

When the physical body dies, our soul moves to another energy plane, where it continues to exist as energy on a higher vibrational level and the harmony and bliss that exists on that plane. The soul will reach one of these energetic planes depending on the soul's development. A soul that has been engaged in self-growth and self-development will reach higher energetic planes and therefore experience a higher level of harmony and bliss while outside the physical plane. The soul will continue to exist until it chooses another physical life circumstance that suits its growth goals and returns to the physical plane once again—back to school.

Our soul, this little drop of the universe's energy that never dies, is really who we are. Our essence is not our physical bodies, minds, brains, looks, profession, career or accomplishments in the physical world. Our essence is our soul, our drop of eternal energy that wants to reunite with the harmony of the vast ocean of the universe's energy.

Why are different people are born into different life circumstances?
When our energy is deciding on a life to embody, it will look to choose life circumstances that have the most potential for learning a specific set of lessons. It is not guaranteed that the life chosen will teach the soul the lessons it came to learn, but it has the potential to do so. Whether the soul learns the lessons it needs to advance to the next level depends on how the person lives their life. That means that when a person goes through life, that life is not wasted if the person connects with their soul, listens to their intuition, and engages in the process of self-growth and self-development to learn these lessons. Connecting to our souls and walking the path of self-realization and self-development will not only bring peace and harmony, but also will enable us to remember the original goals our soul had when choosing these specific life circumstances.

Sometimes a soul will choose to be born into a tough circumstance because it needs to overcome something. Sometimes, it chooses to be born into privileged circumstances because it needs to overcome another issue, like letting go of physical attachments.

No matter the circumstances, the reason is growth and overcoming the things holding it back from ascending to a higher energy level once its body dies. At some point, after many incarnations and lessons learned, the soul reaches the most advanced level and can stay on a higher energetic plane. This plane is pure bliss, love, joy, and harmony. At this point, there is no need to go back to the physical world, which is the lowest level of existence with lots of disharmony and imbalance. Some souls take several lives to learn their lessons before they can remain at a high level and not come back. Other souls require thousands of lives. Nobody really knows because it really depends on what we do during the physical lifetimes and how we use it to grow and develop.

If we live our lives without developing, without connecting to our soul, without connecting to the universe's energy, and only living the physical life, the life is wasted. The soul will have to come back in a similar set of circumstances and relive the experience again and again, until it finally resolves the issues it's meant to learn.

*Karma* is the experiences and issues the soul brings from its previous lives—including the positive and negative energy it has accumulated along the way. All this history can be used and relied upon by connecting to our souls. By learning the lessons our souls need to learn, and developing the things they need to develop, we can remove karma barriers. By removing karma barriers, we do not need to continue working to resolve these issues in future lives. The soul can move on to the next energy level.

Since our souls bring past experiences into each physical life, every person we encounter might have a soul we've encountered before, in a previous life. When this happens, we still have unresolved issues to work out with that soul. The closest people around us have primary karma with us. Which means they are the people we have the most issues to work out with. This could include parents, kids, siblings, etc. Our life partners are also souls we have encountered in previous lives and have unresolved issues to work on with. Uncovering underlying connections with the people in our lives and figuring out the issues we need to resolve with these souls is a highly rewarding experience on multiple levels. Firstly, it focuses us to dig deep into the barriers that could be removed with the closest people in our lives. Once we discover and resolve the issues with these people, karma ends, and we feel enormous relief. The energy from a blossoming relationship can grow to a much higher level and become a much more satisfying relationship. Furthermore, solving karma issues opens an immense *karma bank* of positive energy. Which means there is significant potential for unexpected positive events (in the physical world) that would occur to both souls if they resolved a previous karma barrier with a primary karma soul.

It is important to mention the other side of this. Many people will live their lives without any memory of their soul's purpose. In these cases, life is wasted, and the lessons must be learned in another incarnation.

Furthermore, unfortunately, some people will live their lives in negative energy. This could manifest as physical violence against others or spending life in a constant negative energy. Either scenario will create *new negative karma* within their souls. All this negative karma will have to be worked out and fixed in multiple future lives—some through painful experiences. For example, a person who inflicted violence in one life might be a violence victim in another. Positive energy actions will accumulate as positive karma, resulting in positive experiences. Negative energy actions will accumulate as negative karma that will have to be worked out in future lives—usually through some sort of suffering.

Walk the path that follows the goals and needs of your soul. Doing so will open the door to unexpectedly positive possibilities. Your current physical life could become many times more amazing beyond your imagination. By opening positive "Karma banks" you could achieve and significantly supersede your physical goals as the universe energy will be blowing wind in your sails. Furthermore, using your existing circumstances to self-develop and grow will enable you to close the door on karma issues from your soul's past. Enable your soul to reach higher energetic planes. You'll feel the universe's harmony and bliss.

# PART III: FINDING YOUR PATH TO HAPPINESS

# DESIGNING YOUR LIFE

Life should be treated as a vision board, and you are the designer of it. Most people live their lives as a drifting leaf on a river. The reason being that we are not aware that we have total freedom to design our own lives.

The idea of designing your life is looking at your life as if you are looking at your living space and organizing the furniture in a way that's perfect for you. While everyone understands the need to design living spaces to suit personalities and lifestyle, almost no one understands the need to design their lives to suit their specific personalities and needs.

Most people are sort of floating from one station to another, based on the normal social programming in their society. From grade school to college, from college to work, and so on. They take on a relationship that leads to kids and then retirement. Even the time spent inside each stage is programmed versus planned, so everyone just follows a sequence of events that happens. Not only are these stages not planned by individuals—

even the routes in between the various life stations are programmed by society.

If we remember that our lifetime is limited, and that is the one thing that is 100% guaranteed, we should take the most advantage of it. The same way we want to get the most out of our limited living spaces. So, if we put huge efforts into designing our apartments to be the most pleasurable to spend the time we have in them, why are we not spending the equivalent amount of time and energy into designing our lives? Shouldn't we spend our limited years in the happiest state we can?

No one thinks that designing life is their personal responsibility. Few realize it's even a possibility. Social programming does not encourage or teach it. Instead, everybody is taught to follow the same general path, and this path rarely leads to personal happiness.

Once you are aware of your personal freedom—your ability to design your own path—you can access a whole universe of new possibilities with unlimited prospects for personal happiness and success. Furthermore, when you are free to design and redesign your life continuously, you can change and adjust what works best for you—which continues to constantly improve your life. The beauty of this process is that it can continue as long as you live and therefore your life will continue to improve continuously throughout the whole of your life span.

Like most people, you've probably followed a socially-programmed path: grade school, university, work, marriage, kids, and retirement. You've been taught that this is the only path to a successful life. You want to be successful, and it's easy to follow the crowd. The problem is, of course, that following the flock without personalized adjustments might not work for you—the same way that stuffing your living space with one standard design will not maximize your comfort. Look at the success stories of our generation, people like Steve Jobs, Mark Zuckerberg, and Elon Musk. They designed their lives as opposed to succumbing to social programming.

Once you understand you can customize your life, you can start looking at your personal preferences and views in regard to happiness. For example, choosing what to study in university should be directly connected to your passions and not only to what is considered popular, commonly accepted, or even expected by your family. Many kids end up choosing colleges based on their parents' desires. Even worse, tons choose to study subjects they do not relate to because their parents or social programming dictate following this path. While it is not wrong to continue family traditions or following the socially influenced programs, it is bad if doing so comes at the expense of your personal happiness. Do you want to spend the next sixty years doing something you don't enjoy? Even going to college immediately after high school might not be the best choice for you. Some kids are just not ready. Some need time to decide what they want to study, and some are better off traveling or working. Or on the contrary, some people might want to go to college despite the fact that they might be the first one in their families to do so, and therefore going to college might not be part of their family social programming. Many people choose a career or a workplace that they don't like and enjoy, and once they are in it, they feel trapped to continue following that path due to social programming and various social pressures. In this type of a situation, people might feel trapped in a situation where they are not happy but don't see the possibility and the freedom to restructure their situation. Many time people find themselves in a relationship that does not make them happy, but they might stay in that relationship because its comfortable and/or socially accepted. They don't feel they have the freedom or agency to take charge of their own happiness.

I realize that designing your life could sound like a vague concept. So here are a few suggestions on how to design your life.

The idea is simple. *Customize your life in a way that works for you*. Not only is it okay to question generally accepted lifestyles, but it's also crucial to find your personal way to happiness. Remember that your happiness is *your* responsibility—not your parents, friends, or society. If you do not *own* this responsibility, you will never achieve your best life.

When you examine your life, you'll see that every day you do thousands of small things—most are routines you have been doing for years. If you examine these routines, you'll notice things you never thought about or planned. These routines developed over the years, simply by doing them. Some of the things you do are necessary, like eating, showering, or taking out the garbage. Others are designed to relax, like chilling in front of the tv, having a beer, taking a walk, or spending time with your loved ones. Perhaps you enjoy a hobby or two. Some routines have multiple benefits, like working out, riding a bike, or hiking. In any case, despite the thousands of things you perform each day, you've probably never thought about how much time exactly you want to dedicate to each one of the activities you are performing daily based on the value this activity brings you.

Your initial response might be: *Oh, I really don't have much choice. I need go to work. After work I am tired, and all I want is to relax in front of the tv with a beer or see friends.* But as the designer of your life, you need to realize that everything is a choice, and you are the only one who should decide what to do with your time. If you need money, you know you need to work to get money. If you decide you want more money, then you need to spend more time working at the same job or get another job. These are choices. If you decide you do not want to work for money, you can choose to live off-grid and survive in nature. This choice will completely change the structure of your days.

No matter what you decide to do, you have choices. For example, when you come home from work, you can relax in front of the TV, go to the park, or engage in some kind of sport. Each one of these choices will bring different benefits and value to your life.

The most important thing to understand is that every minute you live, *you should consciously decide* how to spend it. It's in your control to continue spending your time the way you have been or find a better design for your time that will bring more value to your life.

Are you unsure? You are fine anyway, right? You go about your routines. You have fun once in a while, so everything is fine, right?

As the designer of your life, you want to create an environment that is the most conducive to finding your happiness. And it is your responsibility to find and create your own happiness—as it is in your control to do so. The time you spend on various daily activities directly affects the quality of your life and therefore the level of happiness you experience. So, how do you improve the quality of your life?

Look at your daily routines and see how much time you dedicate to the different activities such as work, hobbies, relaxation, socializing, working out, and spending time with your family. Consider the happiness value you derive from each activity. For example, you might not enjoy your working hours, but perhaps you derive happiness value from the money you earn—money that gives you the ability to do other activities, like having the living standard you like. What is the happiness value you get from chilling out in front of the tv? By breaking down each daily activity into a happiness value (direct or indirect), you derive the basic matrix of your life.

Just by doing that, you have already accomplished a major success. You've gained a much better understanding of where you spend your time, and which activities make you happy and bring more value to your life. Maybe you've also learned which activities waste time and do not make you happy.

If you think that earning a lot of extra income makes you happy because you can improve your living standard, and you derive significant happiness value from doing so, then go ahead and work longer hours or invest more time in getting a better paying job. Alternatively, if you think you derive most of your happiness outside of work activities, and the extra income is not adding significant happiness value to your life, then maybe you should work fewer hours and dedicate more time to the out-of-work activities that make you happy. If going to parties and getting drunk means less happiness value compared to spending quality moments at home with a valued person, you might want to cut the number of days you party, or change or diversify your group of friends.

Make a list of all the activities you do during the day for a week and assign a score of one to five based on the happiness value of each. Five being the most and one being the least. By doing so, and looking at the various happiness values, direct or indirect, you can choose to spend more time doing the activities that bring more value to your life.

If you see—based on your evaluation—that career development brings a lot of value since you feel accomplished and make more money to spend, then you can choose to work more hours at that stage of your life. Or, if you notice your current relationship is contributing less value than you thought before rating it, you might consider changing the relationship dynamics or reducing the amount of time dedicated to that specific relationship (I will elaborate more about relationship dynamics in the chapter covering relationships.) Another example could include looking at the amount of time you spend on social media and what value that brings to your life. If your happiness value rating from this activity is low, you might discover you have been wasting a lot of your limited time. Or, for example, if you see that hiking or doing sports scores very high on your list because you enjoy its physical and mental benefits, spend more time doing that. The important point is that *you* are the one to consciously evaluate where your time is best invested.

Everyone is different and will derive different happiness levels from different activities. But the most important thing to remember is that you are in control of the time you spend on the things you do every day. You are responsible for your happiness, and no one else can make you happy. Identify the things that bring you the most happiness value in life and spend more time doing these things. Identify the things that bring less value to your life and spend less time doing these things. Monitor and adjust where needed constantly and continually.

You may have responsibilities you don't enjoy, yet they contribute indirectly to your level of happiness and therefore you need to get them done. For example, you might not enjoy throwing out the garbage, but if you do not dispose of garbage, your living space will smell. When your surroundings become uninhabitable, your level of happiness decreases dramatically. So, taking the garbage out on time contributes indirectly to your level of happiness. You might not want to study for an important exam, but if you don't, you'll reduce the number of opportunities available to you and significantly reduce your level of happiness. Studying for the exam might contribute indirectly to your *future* level of happiness.

The answers are different for each one of us, and that is the beauty of it—we are the designers of our lives!

So, always look at what activities in your life bring you the most happiness value (direct or indirect) and do more of those activities. Monitor the activities that do not contribute to your happiness and spend less time doing these activities. Monitor and adjust constantly. By doing so, you will be a happier person and the designer of your life!

# TRUE FREEDOM

When you realize you have the choice to be free of the social programming and social conventions dictating your life, you have *true freedom*. What does that mean?

We live in a physical world. You go through your daily routines, chasing dreams and goals. You are afraid or anxious about different things, and you dream about accomplishing certain physical goals. But deep inside, what you really want is to find happiness and harmony. One of the milestones on the journey to finding happiness and harmony is finding freedom.

Freedom of what?

The answer is that we need to find freedom from fear, anxiety, anger, disappointment and all the negative background noise and emotions that are constantly circulating in your mind, weighing on you in your day-to-day life.

Most of the people on the planet believe that physical life (our day-to-day life in the physical world) is the totality of our existence. We are so engulfed in our physical lives, and so controlled by our egos, that we don't realize that the physical part of our existence is only a part (a small part) of who we really are. In order to achieve freedom from our fears and anxieties, first we need to understand the totality of our existence.

Our body, mind, and ego are the parts we are the most aware of. These are responsible for daily survival and goals and desires in the physical world. But if that was the total picture, our total existence, then there would be no real purpose to life beyond just existence, and the only thing left would be to struggle through physical life, without any hope for real happiness and purpose. In this type of existence, we would only experience moments of temporary fleeting joy, while most of our time would be a continuous struggle to satisfy one physical desire after another, without any hope of freedom and true happiness. Unfortunately, most of the people on the planet live their lives in this way.

So, what else is there?

Well, the thing we need to understand is that our physical parts, our physical body and physical senses, are only a small part of who we are. This is a big statement, but throughout this book I will go through the various energetic aspects of human beings that most do not focus on or might not even be aware of. The importance of understanding this cannot be underestimated. Knowing this can lead you on the path to finding your happiness and harmony.

Let's start with the understanding that we are not only our physical bodies, but we are also truly energetic beings. What does that mean? It means that beyond your physical body (including your brain), you have an energetic presence. This energetic presence can be difficult to identify, even though it's much bigger than your physical body.

I will expand on these concepts and realizations throughout the book.

If you understand that your existence consists of a combination of your physical body and your energetic body, you will understand the big picture of how these work together.

The first thing to understand is that there are multiple planes of existence. You can look at them as multiple worlds. There is the physical world, which you are familiar with, plus multiple energetic worlds you can't sense through your five senses. These worlds are not part of the social programming, and therefore, we are mostly not aware of them. Because of social programming, our five senses and our egos are only aware of our physical bodies. We are not aware of our energetic presence. As mentioned before, when we are born and through our early childhood, we feel our energetic presence and we are connected intuitively to our souls and the energy of the universe. But because of the continuous social programming we are indoctrinated over the years we disconnect from it and start being controlled by our egos. Our egos block the flow of energy between the universe and our souls.

Remember, your ego is programmed by society. Your desire to act and follow certain social patterns of society, family, schools, friends, and work associates, is programmed into you from birth. As we have already understood, this social programming is designed to keep society functioning but has nothing to do with teaching us to connect to our energetic presence and the energy of the universe.

Beyond social programming, our ego is affected by our desires. Our ego wants to stay in control of us. It wants to direct our physical life. To stay in control, it keeps sending fear and anxiety signals to our body, forcing us to follow its objectives and desires instead of harmony and connection.

Without ego blocking the energy flow to our higher self, you would live your physical life guided by the natural, beautiful, and harmonious flow of the universe's energy. I am not referring to planets and the solar system. When I talk about the flow of the universe's energy, I am referring to higher energetic planes. These higher energetic planes consist of harmonious energy and light. They are void of fear, anxiety, and chaos. These energetic planes are nirvana—just like various writings note. But the most important aspect is that these energetic planes are full of abundant, beautiful, harmonious, and positive energy. Because we have energetic presence, we can tap into that part of ourselves, we can connect with the universe's abundant, harmonious energy. By connecting, we bring the shine of that energy into our physical life—and can truly unlock our internal happiness. We would be able to get rid of fear, anxiety, anger—emotions generated by our ego.

Breaking free from our fears and anxieties is true freedom. This is the reason that many Eastern philosophies and spiritual teachings teach us to understand that if we overcome our ego's generated fears, anxieties, and anger we will become happy and enlightened.

Find your personal nirvana, your inner light. In turn, you will find your inner happiness, which is the deepest level of happiness there is.

The problem, of course, is how to get there. There are many paths and ways, but one way to look at true freedom from fear and anxiety is to understand that the physical world is really just a dream. It isn't real. It feels real, but so does the dream. Paraphrasing my favourite contemporary spiritual teacher, Eckhart Tolle: "When we are dreaming, everything feels real. But when we wake up, we are in a warm bed and we are safe, we are fine." Whatever scared us in the dream was nothing more than part of the dream. From the perspective of our physical mind and body, our physical life is the only reality we have. From the perspective of our soul and energetic body, the physical life is but a tiny part of our existence and experience and can be viewed as a temporary phase, just like a dream. The most important thing that we should understand and remember is that:

*We are energy beings having human experiences, not human beings trying to have spiritual experiences.*

If we understand that we are spiritual beings having human experiences, then we will not be overwhelmed by reality. We will gain freedom. All the things we are so preoccupied by in this physical world are just temporary struggles and represent only a tiny part of our existence. Nothing that happens to us in the physical world can really threaten us as eternal energy beings. If we understand that, we know that the physical life we are currently living, with its beautiful moments and struggles, could be seen like dreaming a dream, and it's a temporary and a small part of our existence. We will always wake up as energy beings. Everything will be fine. On higher energic planes, everything is harmonious, without any negative emotions or struggles. On that level, we experience complete peace in tune with the energy of the universe.

Knowing this, we can live our life as explorers. Live as an explorer who explores new experiences, new places, new feelings, and all the things that the physical world can offer. That is why we are all here. If we live our lives as explorers of experiences, emotions, events, relationships, and all the expressions of the physical world, then we experience the beautiful parts without fear. Even the negative parts, the traumas and hard experiences that feel negative in the physical world, become positive when considered as part of the learning experience, exploration, discovery, and self-development process.

If we can manage to live our lives as if we are exploring a beautiful "hike" in a beautiful place. If our physical life is a beautiful "hike", we will be in peace and harmony with everything we see and encounter along the way during our lives. Other people will be out enjoying their hikes as well. We can hike together, sharing great new emotions and seeing new places. Then some people might go on a separate path and new people join our hike. Friends, partners, lovers, etc., will come and go. Everything is just one amazing hike that we are free to explore and experience without fear. All that is present in our life hike is joy. If we can live like that, we can take advantage of all the beautiful things that the physical world can offer us, while knowing that it's limited, and we will wake up as a beautiful, harmonious energy at some point. Until we experience the physical life again…

We might as well live this dream as though it is joyful—free of anxiety and fear. Because time in the dream is limited and we need to spend it as connected as possible. Whether we are trying to accomplish various physical goals like wealth, scientific achievement, social standing, athletic goals, or just living an ordinary family life, we need to remember to stay connected with our higher selves and the energy flow of the universe. What we do in our current physical life is not important as long as we are connected to our inner selves and therefore with the universe energy and wisdom. This means that "how" we live our current lives is much more important. By connecting with our inner selves, we are able to grow and self-develop as individuals, while enjoying the physical blessings of physical life. By growing and developing we are able to unlock happiness in our current lives, as well as the ability to move higher on the energetic planes as well after our body dies.

I call this *living correctly*, which, to me, means remembering that we are energy beings experiencing temporary human experiences, and we should stay connected with the flow of the universe's energy to achieve true freedom while participating in the theatre of life. Truly understanding this—feeling it—will set us free from suffering.

Remember, as spiritual beings, we go through this temporary human experience to learn. And, as hard as it is to perceive through our programmed Western minds, our physical existence, or what seems, to us, as our total existence, is actually a very small part of our existence. If we want to unlock our true happiness and potential, we need to connect to our full existence, which includes our physical self as well as our energetic self. We should consider the possibility that we are energy, the majority of our consciousness exists and lives on an energetic plane, and we, or just a very small part of us and our energy, comes to this physical world to play in the theatre of physical life. But that is all life is: a theatre. Although it seems very real and all-encompassing, it is only a temporary phase of our existence. We will wake up at the end of our physical lives as beings of energy.

We, as energy entities, never die. Our energy is eternal and large, and only a tiny part is reincarnated into a physical body when we (as higher selves) decide to participate again in the theatre of physical life. Knowing and remembering this will free us from suffering.

I will take a deeper dive into these concepts in other chapters.

# GETTING OUT OF THE FOG

Another part of creating true freedom is getting out of the fog of unhappiness that surrounds you in your day-to-day life. The way you can do this is by following these steps:

Step one is to recognize your situation, which is very simple. The universe doesn't hate you. Nobody is against you. What happened is that you blocked yourself from the light of the universe's energy around you. That is to say, the routine of repeating negative feelings blocked you from feeling the positive energy of the universe. Once you start seeing it, you can ask yourself what you need to do to eliminate the fog.

The next step is to start connecting with the deeper energy that lives deep inside you, which is a small drop of the positive universe's energy that lives in each one of us and that wants to connect to the universe's energy. That energy wants to see the light. By connecting to it, several things will happen. Number one, you will stop generating negative energy that creates more and more negative fog around you. So, instead of generating negative energy, which increases the fog, you will create positive energy that dissipates the fog.

You do this by noticing your negative feelings each time they happen, preferably in real time. When something happens in your daily life that you perceive as negative, you can notice the negative feelings that are immediately generated by your ego. When you become aware of it, whatever the negative perceived situation might be, you don't need to accompany the event with a circular negative feeling. The negative circular loop works as follows: a negative event happens, our ego generates negative emotions, your brain continuously circulates negative thoughts about this event long after the event passed, you are flooded by negative emotions as a result of this. The result of this is a continuous flood of negative emotions which is in many cases disproportionate from the actual event. For example, when you encounter bad traffic and notice the automatic negative feelings generated, like getting angry at other drivers, notice how the emotions, your ego, tries to control you. Try to eliminate these emotions. In the beginning, you will not be able to eliminate the negative reactions you experience. Remember, you have been having the same negative reactions all your life. But by noticing the negative feelings, you will slowly learn how to control and eliminate them. You will, as people say, *become the master of your universe.* Bad traffic will be just that: a few minutes in bad traffic.

By eliminating negative emotions when you encounter small events, you will learn how to control or eliminate negative emotions when you encounter larger hardships—events you really don't like. More importantly, by not allowing negative emotions to control your actions, you will decrease the fog surrounding you. Like everything else in life, the more you do it, the better you will become.

Step two is for you to connect with the universe's energy around you and in you. You can do this through self-meditation, guided meditation, or by being in nature. You can take a few minutes to meditate wherever you are, at work, at home, outside, inside… it does not matter. Just a few minutes or even seconds of you connecting with your inner self will stop the negative circular loop of thoughts. Later, to fully recharge, when you have the chance you could sit by the ocean and watch the waves, or play with your dog. You could walk in the park, surf, or join a team sport. You might find this connection through painting, crafting, writing, or any other creative activity that clears your mind. It can be any activity you deem positive, relaxing, or fulfilling.

When you disconnect from routine negative signals the mind sends you, you start the process of clearing the fog. Your ego routinely sends you signals that you are in distress. To your ego, you are always in some sort of terrible situation. The mind will constantly send you negative messages because the mind is controlled by your ego. When you eliminate the constant negative flow of routine signals from your brain to your body, you eliminate the source of energy for the negative fog around you.

In conclusion, when you understand your modern life creates negative fog around you, you'll see what prevents you from happiness. Set yourself free. See it, and notice what feeds the fog. Negative emotions to routine events are the source, and you can stop feeding the fog. Some people call this *cleaning your aura*. Once you do that, you will see much clearer. You can follow your path to happiness by knowing which actions in the physical world will make your life better.

The fog prevents you from seeing clearly. Without the fog, you can see your paths, both spiritual and physical. Partake in positive activities that help clear the negative fog, like spending time in nature or doing creative activities. Limit the amount of negativity that feeds the fog so you live a better and happy life.

# CONTROLLING YOUR EGO

We have discussed the issues caused by having our egos controlling our minds and our activities and therefore being in charge of our lives. As we have seen, the first step is being aware of the situation.

By being aware of our ego's control and manipulation over our minds, we can work on taking control back. For example, when we notice the ego is generating and running a negative thought process through our minds, we can stop it. We know it has no positive purpose. The ego, of course, will then find another negative thought to cycle through our minds. Eventually, we will start seeing and noticing this on a consistent basis. We'll be able to stop it earlier and earlier each time. Each time we stop it, we become better at doing it. We'll free our minds, our control centres, and stop the circular negative thought process, making room for positive thoughts and energy to enter the mind.

When the ego has less control over the mind (the control centre), our connection to our souls will awaken. The soul will take over the control centre. This, in turn, will open the connection to the universe's energy, and glimpses of internal happiness and harmony will present. This process might take years, or a lifetime, or many lifetimes. But by decreasing the control ego has over our actions, happiness and bliss will increase immediately. Every time we control it, even for a fraction of time, we immediately in that moment improve our lives by welcoming the universe's energy into our lives. This, in turn, shines inside of us—the light of inner happiness. The more we do it, the better we become, and the better our life quality will become.

As we understand this concept and start working on controlling our egos, we might ask ourselves why the energy of the universe is not fully unblocked. Why doesn't the energy of the universe immediately flow and shine as internal happiness?

The answer is that the mind, as the operating system, got used to allowing the ego to take control, instructing it to act in a certain way. The mind developed a habit of responding, reacting, and acting the same way after experiencing the same reactions to situations. The brain developed muscle memory, responding negatively to events. The brain got used to being constantly dissatisfied, because that is what the ego has taught it for years. Even when we eliminate the ego, our minds still follow old ways because of the muscle memory. Although this generates less negative energy, it still blocks the flow of energy from the universe into us. Our minds developed the muscle memory of circulating negative thoughts, over many years and millions of times of it doing the same thing in response to the ego's signals. Whenever the brain is controlled by the ego, a negative fog created by the constant feeling of unhappiness, anxiety, anger, or discomfort created a dense, hard shell to protect the ego.

How do we free ourselves of all this negative energy?

We re-program our brains to stop sending negative emotions and signals to our body every time something is not going according to our liking. This means that we need to start watching our mind activity. We can watch what happens when we see our ego in action, then stop it from taking over. The brain experiences routine negative energy which accumulates through habit. For example, if it feels like a very cloudy day in the mind, the energy flow is blocked, allowing negative emotions to fester. We will need to reduce this fog in order to open the flow of energy. The cloud cover in our minds is created by a negative vibration energy routine. That is created by not being satisfied with things that are happening around us, because there is always something that we want in the physical world, and when it's not happening according to our desires, we are dissatisfied. Something is always not going according to plan, somebody is not doing what they need to be doing, and this constant low vibration discomfort, anxiety, and unhappiness, creates this fog that blocks the flow of the universe's energy. This makes us unhappy. Many spiritual writings identify this as one of the main sources of human unhappiness.

Once we see a cloudy day inside our minds, our goal should be to clear the sky and make it blue. We want to feel inside of us only sunlight and the energy of the universe shining, flowing, and connecting to us and to our bodies through our souls. Constantly doing this will open the internal true happiness that lives within us. Once we start watching this internal sky inside of us, and noticing the clouds of the endless routine thoughts created through the muscle memory and habit of our brains, we will be able to clean those clouds. They are much easier to clean than dealing with the ego, as they are just habitual.

Once we find a way to eliminate ego from taking over and interfering with us and creating negative energy inside of us, it's easier to move the clouds out of our internal sky just by watching. By focusing and envisioning a clear blue sky in our minds, there will be fewer clouds. The fewer clouds we have, the more of the universe's energy we will feel. The more energy we feel, the happier we will be, and the more connected we will feel. This might take time because our minds have gotten used to responding negatively to events around us. As we re-program our minds to respond positively to events around us—watching, focusing, and repeating—we will be able to, eventually, eliminate all clouds in the mind.

If we have issues that need to be dealt with, we will deal with those issues by using our brains as amazing tools. However, we will not be using our minds to generate routine and negative thought loops that create fog. This is what spiritual writings describe as *being here and now*. Being here and now really means that the mind is not producing anything that is not relevant. Our mind fog results from negative thoughts loops that are not relevant. If the mind is like a clear sky, and we eliminate this compulsive, habitual process of producing negative mind fog, then we remain in the here and now, and we can be and do whatever we are doing in the physical world while enjoying the flow of light, energy, and happiness in a state of harmony.

# NOT FIGHTING YOUR EGO

Once we understand that our ego is what blocks us from being able to connect to the light of our soul and to the universe's energy, we might think we need to fight or squash our ego in order to unblock and open the connection. This continuous fight with ego creates flashes of connection when we're able to beat the ego. But if we try to achieve the connection in this way, the struggle will be continuous and constant.

The root of this struggle is the conflict between our soul, that wants to connect to the energy and light of the universe, and the ego, which is trying to maintain the control over us and our minds. Our soul wants to connect as much as possible to, and to spend as much time as possible being connected to. the energy of the universe because this connection is happiness and harmony, while the ego is constantly blocking this connection in order to stay in control.

This fight with the ego could be won or lost depending on the person. In my case, fighting with the ego just created cycles of light and darkness and I was never able to completely win the fight. The light was coming through when the ego was less strong, but then the ego would become strong and block the light again. This on and off connection would not allow me to feel the light of energy and happiness flowing all the time.

I had to find another path to open the light of energy. For me, the answer was treating my ego with love and compassion. Our ego is an entity which is living in us and it's a part of us. This entity has been created over our whole lifetimes. We can look at our ego like a stray cat. If you fight it, it becomes very aggressive. If it feels threatened, it will fight back. It will bite and scratch. When the ego is bigger and stronger than you, it's no longer a cat, it's a tiger; a tiger that is very aggressive. It's hard to win a fight with that tiger inside of you. Some people even have dragon-sized egos.

But if you show ego that there is no need to fight—if you love your ego—you can share the positives of opening the light of energy and feeling that light with ego. You become partners. Then, this huge, aggressive tiger becomes a kitten who purrs. Ego can enjoy the love it never had, the compassion that it never felt, and understand it doesn't need to fight when there is nothing to fight about. It gets calm once it feels love, compassion and gratitude. It doesn't feel threatened or the need to fight. When it doesn't want to fight, it will not block the light of the universe in you. Ego will not block the universe's energy when its survival is no longer dependent on staying in control.

You can love your ego the same way you love your partner. You can feel compassion and love towards your ego, and it will reciprocate. It will simply enjoy the light you're sharing with it. When ego isn't aggressive or angry, then there is nothing wrong with it. It wants and gets the same things you want: light and the right to exist. Share whatever light you get from the universe with your ego. By doing so, you create love, compassion, and partnership with your ego. It is the alchemy of transforming a relationship from negative enemies and opponents, to partners and best friends.

# LIVING YOUR LIFE CONSCIOUSLY AND ARTISTICALLY

What does it mean to live our lives consciously and artistically?

While we are living our lives in the physical world, we are mostly focused on our daily routines. Some of those routines we like, and many we don't. Most of them are just technical things we do to survive or get to our next vacation or time to relax. This is a loop, and almost every human being on this planet, with a few exceptions, is on this ride continuously and unconsciously. The *art of living* says that this should not be the case.

The art of living says that by being conscious of ourselves and all our activities at any given moment and being connected with our inner selves at any given moment, the result will be a completely different and much more positive and happy life. Sounds good, but how do we do it?

Firstly, whatever we are doing, even if we are doing something routine and technical, we can make it conscious—be aware of the activity we are performing at any given moment. By making even routine actions conscious, we will better understand whether we really want and need to perform these actions at all. For example, we might discover that we are spending five hours a day going through our social media feeds. If we are unconscious about doing it, we might not be aware we are spending that amount of time on this activity. It is part of our daily unconscious routines. Once we notice it, and it becomes a conscious action, we might decide that it does not bring us much value. Being conscious allows us freedom of choice. Once we are conscious and aware of our activities, we have the freedom to choose whether to continue doing it or change it. When we do the same actions and routines unconsciously, we deprive ourselves the chance to choose and design the path of our lives. Once we look at our daily routines and identify the activities that do not add value to our lives, we can choose to stop doing them or reduce the time invested in them.

There are many activities in our daily routines that we need to do in order to make our lives functional. Some of those activities we need to do even if we don't like doing them. By being conscious and present even in those activities, we can make these activities part of our self-growth. Many tasks we *must* execute, like going to work every day, cleaning the apartment, grocery shopping, or studying for exams. We have chosen this specific life structure and in order to make life functional and better, there are certain activities that must come with it. There are certain things we must do even if we do not like to, but we have a choice of how we feel about doing these activities. By changing the way, we feel about activities we don't like to do, we can make them a part of our spiritual growth. By changing our thoughts from "I hate this activity" to "this activity is something I want to do to improve my life quality", we are able to reprogram our minds from generating negative thoughts and vibrations to positive ones. For example, while cleaning, instead of running a loop of negative thoughts like *I do not enjoy cleaning*, try to be present in the task. Focus on the physical task without running any negative thought loops. By doing so, the mind is cleared. And, by focusing on the actual physical task being performed, a state of meditation is reached.

This understanding allows us to see that it is our conscious choice to live the life structure we have chosen. We are free to change our life structure, even the routines, if we feel that change will bring more happiness. But, while we are performing the routines in our current life structure, we should be present and conscious while doing them. As Eckhart Tolle says, even the mundane things that we are doing, we can do in a way that is not mundane. By performing our routines with this mindset, we establish a connection with our inner selves. The more we are conscious about our day-to-day activities—accept them as necessary parts of our lives—the more we enjoy the mundane things while doing them. Being present and focused without continuous, negative thought loops, can create a stronger connection between our soul's energy and the energy of the universe.

Furthermore, when we are conscious and aware of our routine daily activities, we have the freedom to design our lives. We should design our lives the same way we would design things in the physical world, like our homes. Our lives should not be designed by random circumstances—we are the masters and designers of our lives. It is our responsibility to structure our lives in a way that is best for us. Each and every one of us should decide what value every part of our life and our actions has. Each action we perform should add a positive value to our life—whether physical, energetic, or emotional. For example, when we go to work, there is value in receiving money, a sense of self-accomplishment, and, if we like our jobs, a positive time spent performing it. If we are in a positive relationship, we get the value of positive emotions like love and connection. If we engage in sports, we get the value of physical health and enjoyment of the sport. On the other hand, as mentioned before, some activities do not offer any positive value, like spending time being angry or gossiping.

We need to understand that we have the choice to live our lives in an artistic and self-designed way that works for us. Then we can compare the life we are living to a potential life we want to design for ourselves. This will enable us to make changes in various aspects of our life that do not correspond to our properly designed life. These changes will improve the physical quality of the life we will be living, and of course our level of happiness.

By being conscious while going about our daily routines and improving the connection with our souls and the universe, we can turn the life we choose into a spiritual practice that will result in internal happiness. A spiritual practice, in this context, means that we are aware and conscious of our routines, daily activities, and we understand the positive value each brings to our lives. Activities that do not add positive value to our lives are eliminated or reduced. Activities that add positive value to our lives, we try to do more of. We are present and focused.

By combining the above concepts, we live the best possible life that we can imagine for ourselves. By being conscious and aware, we introduce freedom of choice into our lives. We are responsible for choosing which activities and routines are part of our lives. And the routines we choose will be our gateway to self-growth and inner happiness.

# COMFORT ZONES

Most people live their lives inside of their *comfort zones*. This is very logical. As the name implies, every comfort zone consists of an environment and situation that is familiar and comfortable for us. Normally, comfort zones are not constructed by people, as part of their life's design, but by the sum of people's day-to-day routines. These routines could be good or bad, and, in most cases, are just average, grey routines. Nevertheless, they provide people with a familiar environment and structure that creates a mental psychological comfort level. Interestingly, even bad circumstances can be a comfort zone for people due to sense of familiarity.

If comfort zones provide a feeling of comfort, what is the problem?

The problem is that there is no new information and possibilities inside of our existing comfort zones. In order to improve and achieve our best lives we need to constantly self-develop and improve in the areas that are important to us, whether it's our careers, relationships or finding happiness. This means that we need to go outside of our comfort zones to achieve this development. There is no possibility for any personal development and growth inside of one's comfort zone. By definition, a comfort zone is created by routine. This routine is the sum of all the familiar activities a person performs on a day-to-day basis. Meaning that most people don't consciously design their daily routines and comfort zones, they just happen by themselves over the years. If a person lives their entire life inside their comfort zone, that person is not experiencing personal growth or personal development. If there is no personal growth and development, then there is no possibility of maximizing our life potential and finding the path for our true inner happiness and best life.

Not only are comfort zones constructed of daily routines, but the activities also happen unconsciously. Almost no one designs or structures their daily routine in a way that maximizes their personal happiness and growth. Most people just follow the path that everyone in their surroundings is following and normally are programmed to follow by the society. Therefore, it's realistic to say that many people live in comfort zones that would not maximize their potential for the best life they can live. Therefore, most comfort zones are not designed and do not allow people to achieve their true potential or find happiness.

As discussed before, for a person to achieve true happiness and their true potential, they need to be on a path of self-development and self-growth. For a person to achieve their true potential in physical aspects like career, wealth, academia, or athletic achievements, requires self-development and constantly improving in these areas.

If a person is living inside their comfort zone, with no new information or circumstances getting inside, there is absolutely no growth in the physical areas that are important for the person i.e. career, relationships, family, as well as personal development. The only possibility is routine stagnation. Psychologically, we feel very comfortable staying inside our comfort zones. But, if we consider the ramifications of stagnation, we'd realize that living inside a comfort zone is an impediment to success and happiness.

How do we break free from our comfort zones?

The good news is that to accomplish growth, success, self-development, and happiness, we do not need to completely break free from our comfort zones—and definitely not in one shot. We can slowly venture outside our comfort zones to gather new information and experience new circumstances. We can start doing this in the areas most important to us. For example, if we are interested in improving our financial situation, we can wander outside our comfort zone to identify new business or career opportunities—maybe even new paths that change our mindset. The important thing is to go beyond and outside of our comfort zone into areas not considered before, even if the experience is temporarily uncomfortable. If we want to explore new relationships, we will need to examine new ways to engage, communicate, and spend time with people.

We do not have to go too far away from our comfort zones all at once, we can do it in small steps. As we start venturing outside our area of comfort, we will discover new opportunities and new ideas. Some we will like, and some will not suit us. We can expand further on the ones that feel promising and interesting, and not pursue the ones that don't fit. Slowly, we can venture further and more often. Each time we leave our comfort zone, we expand our universe and open new possibilities for growth. And self-development will lead to improved lives and happiness. We will also find that as we start searching outside our comfort zones, the universe will start presenting us with new opportunities. The universe responds positively to efforts of personal growth and development.

The more we venture outside old comfort zones, our new comfort zone will grow. The bigger the comfort zone, the bigger the universe of possibilities. The bigger the universe of possibilities, the more chances of success—physical and spiritual.

This process is no different than going to a gym to work out. The more we work out, the more weight we can lift, and the higher the level of workout we can do. Working out is not easy while we are doing it, but it offers benefits like improving our physical conditioning and mental wellbeing. Going outside a current comfort zone is not easy, but it increases the possibilities for greater things. Every successful individual, whether in business, art, sports, or spiritualty, had to go outside their comfort zone in order to achieve something extraordinary. While not everybody wants to accomplish and experience extraordinary things, in order to experience and achieve anything extraordinary, we need to go outside our comfort zones.

Even if happiness is the only goal, we need to exit our comfort zone to achieve happiness.

As we start experimenting with going outside of our own comfort zone, how do we know whether we ventured out of it? The simple answer is that whenever we leave our comfort zone, no matter in what area, we will feel uncomfortable in the beginning. This feeling of discomfort should not hold us back, on the contrary, this can be our sign that we are outside of our normal comfort zone. Once we start to experiment with the new information and possibilities outside of our comfort zones, we can decide what works for us and what doesn't. In areas that we have discovered work for us outside of our previous comfort zones, we can expand our search and in areas that we see that don't work for us, we can decide not to venture further.

The bottom line is, to achieve our full potential we can't hide inside comfort zones. Depending on our personal goals, we need to venture outside our comfort zones to learn, grow, and explore possibilities. The most developed people might not need a comfort zone at all. For them, the whole universe is as comfortable as their daily routine. In any case, the more we experiment with expanding our comfort zones, the more potential we will have to find and live our best lives as well as finding our path to happiness.

# DECISION MAKING

Every decision we make opens a new path of possibilities. Every decision is a new path on the decision tree, and every new path on the decision tree is a whole new branch leading to completely different life possibilities. Meaning, every decision, small or large, has the potential to lead our life circumstances in a completely new branch on the decision tree of our lives. It does not make it good or bad, but it makes it very interesting to understand how to make decisions and what consequences our decisions have, whether they be good or bad. Our lives are constructed from millions or even billions of decisions. Most of them are small, some are big, and some seem small but are actually big. In any case, during our lives we need to make many, many decisions.

Most of the decisions we make do not require much thought. They are small decisions, so we just do it, which is fine because they don't have significant ramifications. When we are faced with what we consider to be big decisions, most people apply logical thinking to their decision making, like making a list of pros and cons.

Any decision can have a dramatic effect on our life's course. Because each decision creates a new path on the decision tree, like a branch on a tree that grows into another branch. Each decision creates a completely new decision tree branch of opportunities. Eventually, the place we end up in is completely different from where we would end up if we had made a different decision at the beginning of the branch. When we consider that each direction is actually a full set of events we live through, we understand that even a small decision creates a completely new set of circumstances—positive or negative.

Knowing the importance of every decision, how do we move forward?

Firstly, we should be aware of the significance of our day-to-day decision making. Our choices have significant ramifications for our lives—even though they might not seem to when we are making them. In most cases, we can't perceive the future tree branches that will be created or missed by making certain decisions. But, if we are cognizant of this fact, we might have a better chance to be as smart as we can.

Secondly, it is very important, especially for the bigger decisions, that we use our intuition as part of the decision-making process. Because our intuition will give us higher chances of choosing the right decision that will lead us to maximizing our life's potential, both spiritually and physically. For example, deciding to marry someone is a big decision. Normally. Most people would apply a combination of logic and emotion. From the logical point of view, they would think whether this person is who they are looking for or not, based on a perceived list of attributes their perfect match should possess. From an emotional point of view, they would question whether they were in love with this person, and, if not, wonder what other emotions they feel. In most cases, the decision to marry is made by using the above two tools. Although marriage is one of the most important decisions a person will make, in most cases, people will not consciously add the third tool to the decision-making process: intuition. Adding intuition means listening to our inner voice (not our minds) regarding how we feel when we're with that person. Does coming together create positive energy and a feeling of positive potential, or just a routine feeling or some sort of a discomfort? In order to listen to our intuition, we need to go deep into ourselves and quiet our minds. The sense that will emerge from that will give us an indication regarding our intuition about that subject. When we combine all the tools we have, we can make the best decisions.

Any important decision could potentially have very significant ramifications on one's direction in life, quality of life, and accomplishing one's potential and goals in life. Moving yourself above the normal, physical decision-making process, and trying to connect with your intuition to improve the quality of your decision, would be very useful in addition to logic and emotions.

What is interesting is that in many of the decisions we make, we don't realize that by choosing to do something or not to do something, we are either losing the potential or gaining the potential for something big to happen.

Decision making also connects to one's karma. For example, you might have a new person in your life romantically. You feel an attraction to this person, and are not sure why, but something in your intuition feels a pull to that person. But technical circumstances make it difficult to follow-up, so you don't, thinking it's not important. *This is just one suiter and there will be more.* In reality, this one decision might lead you to miss a significantly important partner the universe has sent your way. By ignoring your intuition, you might have missed an amazing relationship that could have been built from the initial physical attraction. And don't forget karma. There might have been a karmic connection from a previous life—the possibility of enjoying a relationship with a much higher connection level.

Maybe you meet someone professionally and feel a connection with the person. Again, due to technical difficulties, you don't bother to follow-up on this connection. You will never know if that person might have been a potential partner in a new business, or if the universe and karma brought you the opportunity. Perhaps the person's karma combined with yours would have resulted in success beyond your imagination. Together, you might have had the potential to build a successful business, but by passing on the opportunity, the potential is lost. The universe might not offer a similar opportunity again. The same situation could happen with a career opportunity you have encountered, that you felt good intuition about, but didn't follow through due to technical difficulties, and therefore missed out on a whole promising career path that might have opened up for you.

The important point to understand and consider here is that the universe offers amazing opportunities connected to karma. When you feel a certain pull towards a person or an opportunity, and you need to decide whether to pursue it or not, you should remember that not pursuing the direction your intuition is pushing for, might have significant ramifications. This also works in the opposite direction. If you feel your intuition signalling you to stay away from a certain person or opportunity, and you ignore it, there might be negative consequences.

Remember, every decision leads to another decision and a new branch of events. Each branch on the decision tree consists of events that are completely different. Your circumstances change dramatically with every decision you make, and new branches develop every time you make a choice. But this should not paralyze you or prevent you from making decisions. On the contrary, you should be excited by the opportunities the universe can offer. Use *all* the tools at your disposal, including your mind, emotions, and intuition. Doing so will help you find the path with the most potential to reach your life's goals.

# RELATIONSHIPS

Almost every human being on this planet is preoccupied, at one time or another, with relationships. So, let's discuss dating and looking for a partner in the modern world from an *energy* standpoint.

As discussed before, social convention dictates that everybody should follow the same path in life. When it comes to relationships, this means that everyone follows the same relationship goals as well as the same process of finding and structuring our relationships. People are constantly searching for their life partners by going on dates and following the same socially-programmed paths without thinking whether these work for them. No one wonders if this process makes them happy. Sometimes, the goals of the dating process are not even clear. Once in a relationship, most people again follow social models and fall into the same routines programmed into them since birth. Let's unpack these misperceptions to understand them from a non-scientific point of view.

Why do most modern-day relationships not bring you the promised satisfaction you so desire? And what do you do about it?

The conventional relationship path, in its most basic form, tells you to find a man or woman you will eventually marry, you have kids, get a dog and live happily ever after. You eventually die together, ideally in your nineties, while holding hands and watching the sunset. This is what a relationship looks like based on what works best for society. In societies, it is important that people get married and produce children, as these grow the nation and increases productivity in terms of workforce and the number of taxpayers. It is also important for society to keep families in an organized, stable structure, so children are raised to be contributing members of society. These factors are very important from the standpoint of society, and why we are programmed from childhood to follow these steps. But these steps are not necessarily good for your individual happiness.

For many people, this structure will not correspond with achieving personal goals or individual happiness, as it was not designed for that. Evidence for this is today's high divorce rates. In some countries, over fifty percent of the population finds themselves trapped in a relationship structure that does not work for them. On top of that, many of the people who don't get divorced are unhappy—in many cases miserable. Most are afraid of the negative technical ramifications of getting a divorce, like the potential effects on kids, fear of being alone, being afraid of leaving their comfort zone, or financial consequences. If we combine these two numbers together, we see that the majority are following a socially-programmed path that does not work for them.

Despite knowing everything said above, most will get married and divorced, suffering enormous emotional, economic, and physical stress in the process.

This concept applies to everything you do in your life. Societies have very clear directions for how people should structure their families. Even religions require a specific family structure to keep people compliant with their needs and demands. Your parents, who do their best and love you the most, have been indoctrinated with the same structures. They were never taught to think about their happiness, so they just led you the same way they were unconsciously led by their parents.

As crazy as it sounds, we are following social programming that has a very low probability of success. Odds are, following suit will cause us tremendous stress. But this is only because we are not aware of other options.

Almost no one considers alternative relationship structures before they start dating. Few dwell on how a relationship might contribute to their personal happiness. We all just follow the standard structure—only to discover later that this one-size-fits-all structure does not work. Even when people discover that the social structure does not work for them, in many cases, they do not realize they have the freedom to create their own relationship structure based on their individual needs.

We are programmed by social norms to walk like sheep, following one other without seeing where we are going or why. We do not see the bigger picture, our happiness. We only see the sheep in front of us, and that sheep sees only the sheep in front of it. If the first sheep falls of a cliff, the others follow, not because it's good for them or because it will lead them to happiness (which it might), but because none of them saw the bigger picture. They didn't question the path or consider the possibilities.

What is the solution? The answer is that it depends on us. We are all different, and we have different needs. Our individual path might be completely different from the standard path of society, or it might be similar. The most important thing to understand is that in order to achieve happiness, we need to structure our lives to accomplishes personal goals and pursue happiness. If we understand that creating happiness is our *responsibility*, and no one else can give it to us, we will understand that we need to choose our own path. When we choose our own path to happiness, we set goals and design our lives accordingly.

The key to finding happiness is to understand we have options to structure our lives and relationships in a way that works for us. You are an individual with different needs, personality, goals, and development levels. Why would we expect that following someone else's structure would make us happy? We should choose a structure that works for us and our partners, regardless of what your social programming dictates. By doing so, the probability we'll achieve a beautiful relationship and/or happiness will increase dramatically. Both on an individual level and a couple level. This process of de-programing would increase your probability of happiness in every area of life.

We have total freedom over your own life. We are responsible for our happiness and we are free to design and structure our relationships in a way that will bring us joy and happiness. You can choose to live your life based on social convention if you understand it's a conscious choice because you feel that is where your happiness is. On the other hand, you can choose a completely different life structure if you feel that the socially-accepted relationship structure is not for you. It does not matter what type of structure we choose. What is important is that *we* have chosen it based on our individual needs, goals, and happiness.

The choices never end. Our path towards happiness is a process of re-programming and self-growth. We might discover that the path we initially thought was the right choice doesn't work for us anymore. We can constantly adjust our path based on self-growth, development, and the world around us. There is no obligation to choose one direction and never correct our course. As long as we aim for happiness and fulfilment, we have a much better chance of achieving both.

Once we understand there is more than one way to live life, and that our happiness is dependent on finding the specific structure that works for us, we can make a conscious choice whether to follow the social programming or not. Either one is good as long as we chose it as our own conscious path to our happiness. This is basically taking the blindfold off our eyes, which kept us following other people. Start looking for, and analyzing, what type of relationships you want—what makes you happy. We can choose a mate or decide to stay single. We can get married or live as a couple without getting married. You can have a monogamous or non-monogamous relationship. You can have children or not have children. You can live in a normal social setting or choose to live off-grid in the nature. There are endless choices and structures to choose from.

We can also look at the way we choose our life partners. When we look to meet *the love of our life*, we create a fantasy description in our mind—an array of perfect images and scenarios we believe are ideal. But these are built from a combination of desires and social programming. Our mind is used to wanting things from a very young age. Our wants are connected to other things in our personality, society, and geography. Some of our wants are based on basic needs like food, shelter, and security, but most are desires based on social programming, like money, success, fame, social standing, etc. Our mental desires are based on how we compare ourselves to other people such as family, neighbors, peers, or friends. Our desires are basically our mind's translation of the social programming we have absorbed over our life and how we see ourselves succeeding based on those social programs. The issue with this is that these desires have little to do with our actual needs and even less to do with happiness. We are constantly evaluating our world based on programmed desires, not personal needs. In fact, most of the needs that would lead to happiness are ignored.

Many times when a socially-programmed person arrives at a first date, instead of being in the moment and allowing himself/herself to be open to the opportunity the universe has presented, he/she is totally engulfed in measuring the date in comparison to the socially-induced fantasy. And in the process, could totally be missing the opportunity that is in front of him/her. The opportunity in front of him/her will always be different from his/her fantasy, and, in many cases, could be better than his/her fantasy, as the universe always sends exactly what we need. If person is too busy staying inside their locked and programmed mind, trying to force fantasy onto reality, they will not even see the possibilities in front of them.

This is not to say that every person you meet will be the right person. This is the purpose of dating, to see if you are interested or not interested in starting a relationship. But if we want to explore the opportunities the universe brings to us, then we might want to disconnect from our pre-conceived and pre-programmed mindset when meeting someone new. Listen to our intuition. As noted before, society's pre-programmed concepts are likely to fail anyway. But our intuition, free of programing, has the potential to find the path that works for us. Therefore, if we remain open to all possibilities when we meet a new person, and allow our intuition—not our programming—to guide us, we are more likely to find the right partner for us and our combined happiness. And, if we structure our relationship in a way that works best for us and our partner, based on intuition and communication and without being prisoners to social programming, we can build a relationship that leads to happiness. In the end, our happiness depends on our individual choices.

The universe will only offer what we really need; then it is our choice what to do with it. Look at everything that happens to you with an open mind, trying to understand the opportunities in front of you. To truly do it properly, you need to disconnect from what you think that you desire and look at everything with a fresh set of eyes. This is very difficult as it contradicts basic habits we have developed over many years. Furthermore, to appreciate and take advantage of the opportunities the universe presents, you need to go outside your comfort zone.

# RELATIONSHIP FOUNDATIONS

Relationships can be built on many different foundations, like common interests, physical attraction, similar culture and background, common goals, ideals, comfort level, the feeling of security, and so on. The most common foundations are common interests and goals, physical attraction, and the feeling of comfort. When a couple is still in their *falling in love* phase, it is enough to have one or two connection points to feel completely satisfied. Love creates a heavenly feeling that engulfs a relationship in the moment. In this period, partners have no flaws, or, more accurately said, the flaws can't be seen. Everything is viewed through love's lens of perfection. But after some time, when love dissipates, issues with the partner and relationship become clear. Every relationship experiences that, and everyone that has been in love, has felt it. So, what happens when the relationship becomes more mature and is not blinded by the *we are totally in love* aura?

At this point, everything depends on the foundation of the relationship. A relationship that was built purely on physical connection will quickly dissipate and become unsatisfactory. A relationship that was built on common interests and a similar culture might last longer. It is possible that a relationship that is built on common goals will be satisfactory for a relatively long time, as common goals allow the couple to feel satisfied with the relationship for longer. The wider the foundation, and the more common ground it has, the more chances the relationship will be successful and last longer. But even with a very wide foundation, many relationships fail. Why is that the case?

There are endless scientific studies on this topic. It's a universally common issue. I will not get into any of these scientific explanations, but rather look at it from a completely different angle. I will attempt to look at it from the energy standpoint. In my opinion, the quality of a relationship's foundation is dependent on the growth and development of the individuals in the relationship. As the time goes by, each partner will evolve and grow in a certain direction, or not evolve and grow at all.

Let us examine the possibilities. The first option is that each person evolves and grows, but they evolve in different directions. This means that the common interests that the couple might have had are not common any more as each one of them evolved and changed their set of interests. In this case, the foundation, like enjoying the same activities or being interested in the same ideas, is no longer there. In this case, the couple might continue the relationship based on physical attraction or staying in their comfort zone. Physical attraction is a flimsy foundation for a couple. While it can be strong and satisfying in the beginning of a relationship, over time it loses its intensity and appeal, and if not developed and worked on, can disappear altogether. In this case, it is likely that the relationship will end or become an unhappy relationship.

The second option is that one of the partners evolves and grows while the other one does not. The outcome of this will be similar to the previous one. Because in this case as well, the common goals will not be a foundation for the relationship anymore.

The last option is where both partners in the relationship do not evolve or grow. This is an interesting case. In this case, theoretically, the original foundation still exists, so the couple should continue to work well as a couple. But, in most cases, this does not work, because the physical connection is usually lost or reduced significantly. When this happens, common ground holds the couple together—the couple's comfort zone. This is also flimsy and mostly unsatisfying, but a common reason why people stay in relationships.

Let's examine the comfort zone aspect of relationships. On the one hand, it could be viewed as positive. What is wrong with feeling comfortable in a relationship? Many couples, after being in a relationship for a while, will lose the foundation that connected them. Sometimes they are not interested in the same activities anymore, they do not have common goals anymore, or the physical attraction is not as strong as it was before. The only thing that remains is their feeling of comfort. But when the main connection point in a relationship is comfort (their comfort zone), the relationship falls stagnant, becoming unfulfilling in the best-case scenario and negative in the worst case. When the only foundation left is comfort, there is no generation of new positive energy in the relationship. New positive energy and emotions are not generated from common goals or activities, or from the other previously enjoyed foundations.

Many people stay in relationships because one or both partners are afraid to leave their comfort zone. Even if the relationship is unfulfilling or full of negative emotion, the fear of leaving or being alone prevents people from moving on. Some will stay due to financial worries, and some feel they might not find another partner.

There are several issues in this type of situation that are worthwhile looking into. First, the fear of being alone. Many people are instinctively afraid of being alone for even short periods of time. They might not think about the reason and just have an instinctive fear of solitude. These people look to be in a relationship constantly. If a relationship ends, they must find a new one immediately. People who feel this way might stay in negative relationships or will jump into a new relationship even if it is not a positive one. In both cases, the situation is negative. If people would only be more aware of this behavior and look a little deeper into themselves, they would find that this instinctive fear is not justified. And spending time alone is better than being in a negative relationship.

Once this fear loses power, people can find much better, fulfilling, and positive relationships because they will not be under pressure to jump into the first relationship that comes along. Also, when someone takes a deeper look inside, self-improvement can rule. There are several benefits to this sort of self-growth. By being comfortable alone, a person has the freedom to choose between being in a relationship or not. And if a relationship ends, the person will not be afraid of being alone again until they decide when is good for them to start a new relationship and what kind of a relationship they are looking for to maximize their our happiness.

I am not saying that it is better to be in or out of a relationship, but what is important is the freedom to choose. And we get this freedom by being equally comfortable being by ourselves or in a relationship.

Social programming suggests that each one of us is a half looking for the other half to fulfill us. Social programming teaches us to find our 'other half'. There are endless songs and movies that talk about the pain of being only a half of something. We are told we cannot be happy and fulfilled without the half missing from our lives. While there are benefits to sharing life's moments with someone special, this should not be confused with *needing* a missing component. Each one of us is a full human being completely capable of finding our own happiness without another person. In fact, our inner happiness will always be deeper and more fulfilling than any moments spent with the most amazing partner.

Once we understand that we are complete on our own, then we will find the right partner. This will not come from dependance, but from a complimentary point of view. Not from a need but from a life enhancement. This can enable us to choose the right partner to share beautiful moments with, or to choose when we want to be by ourselves. Choice gives us the freedom to be the best version of ourselves, and to live the best life we can live.

If we approach our relationships from the stand point of our growth and happiness as our goals, and start thinking of what works for us personally, we might discover that a good relationship can enhance and support our personal growth—spiritual and physical. When two people grow together, they find happiness as individuals and as a couple. When this happens, everything else, like mutual activities, common interests and physical attraction is enhanced much more. Once we see this, we can start living and experiencing life as a much happier couple. That opens the possibility for us to grow inside the relationship, and to new heights of happiness.

Looking deeper at this foundation point for a great relationship, we will discover this is mostly ignored or overlooked in modern relationships. Each relationship has the potential to be a positive environment in which both people can grow and develop. What this means is that when two people in a relationship are aware of their personal self-development and growth as individuals, they can use the special energy created to boost and grow. At the same time, by developing as individuals, and supporting each other, they grow as a couple as well. By growing as individuals in the frame of a couple that is growing and developing in the same direction, multiple benefits are created.

Self-growth and development are endless and can be a continuous common goal and foundation for a couple. This is by far the deepest foundation a couple can share. The deeper the foundation, the stronger the relationship becomes. Furthermore, by developing together, both partners become better and happier individuals, and the couple becomes a better and happier unit as a result. When a couple has kids, the kids will also feel and absorb and thrive on this positive energy.

If a couple can combine common interests and activities, physical joy, emotional chemistry and support, and self-growth, the potential for an amazing, positive, fruitful, and long-lasting relationship would be beyond anything imaginable.

# BREAKUPS

Breakups from romantic relationships are complicated and emotionally charged. We all feel pain from a breakup because the energies of our two bodies are disconnecting and that is painful. On top of it, the ego starts creating stories around the breakup, like what we are missing, what we're not getting anymore, and what we have lost. These stories create suffering beyond the pain. The ego constantly circulates and continually spins pain in our minds, and that creates more suffering.

The reason romantic breakups feel so painful is because they normally include three layers of pain and suffering. First, there is emotional pain caused by a lack of love. The second layer is the disconnection of energetic bodies that were previously connected. The third is the ego running endless circles of negative thoughts regarding the breakup and ex-partner. While the first two cause temporary pain, the third one creates permanent suffering, as long as the ego continues to run negative thought circles.

Now, everybody experiences breakups. Every beginning has an end, and all relationships end one way or another—by separation or death of the physical body. So, what is the best way of dealing with a breakup?

The first thing to understand is that pain will always be there, especially in the beginning, when you're separating and disconnecting energy fields, shared activities, and joint routines. Since some of these were positive experiences you enjoyed doing with your ex-partner, the emptiness will cause pain. The level of pain depends on the relationship's connection. But while temporary pain is necessary in the beginning, long-term suffering is created by the ego, and is definitely not necessary. Often, the ego is not willing to accept the breakup. The ego will continue spinning negative thoughts loops, which in turn will continue to create unnecessary suffering. This commonly practiced ego spinning converts what should be a short pain cycle into a much longer process of suffering. Every breakup will have a temporary component of pain that will dissipate and disappear over time, but the suffering component is voluntary—and you can save yourself.

How? Try simply noticing the thoughts that come to your mind regarding the breakup, thoughts like:

- I miss that person
- I miss the activities we used to do together
- I miss the love I used to get from that person

- I can't believe that person left me
- I can't believe the relationship ended after everything we experienced together
- That person doesn't deserve me
- I hate that person
- That person is a jerk (or worse)

Thoughts like these come from your ego not accepting the reality of the situation, which is the relationship has ended. Your ego spins negative stories to get you to identify with the pain again and again, thus creating endless, and not needed, suffering. By noticing it, you will not allow your ego to extend the suffering, which will drastically reduce the amount of suffering you need to go through.

Once you understand where negative thought processes originate, concentrate on your energy level. Everything that happens in life, happens for a reason, and everything in the physical world (including our bodies), has a beginning and an end. Relationships, no matter how important or how attached you were to them, will end one way or another, by breakup or death. If the relationship has come to an end, there was an energetic reason for it.

A breakup means two people could not continue to be positive partners on life's journey—even when the technical reasoning behind the breakup isn't clear. You might understand the energetic and karmic reasoning for *the end* sometime in the future, but, at the time, it was enough to understand the relationship's energy was ending.

When the energy of any relationship or process or event ends in the physical world, it is *good*, because the end suggests there was nothing positive. Programmed egos will always try to make the breakup a negative event. But don't forget: The universe always brings you exactly what you need, even when your ego dislikes it. And, if the universe always brings you what you need, then the breakup is the best thing for you. Take advantage of whatever the universe brought you in order to grow and develop as a person and achieve your full potential. Every closed door (in the universe) opens another door, and most times the change is better and more profound. Find the next door. Move forward on your path of development and growth.

The pain you feel from a breakup is only relevant in your physical form, where your consciousness rules. If you're able to move your consciousness into your energetic body—your higher consciousness—then you won't have any pain at all. You will understand that it's meaningless. You will not feel pain because pain is only on the physical, human level. On the energetic level, there is no pain. Everything happens for a reason and the universe is a continuous flow of energy. Therefore, the events happening in the physical world are part of that flow, regardless how they are perceived by our little minds and egos. If, when you feel pain, you move your consciousness higher, connect with the universe's energy and light, the pain will go away. From the universe's standpoint, nothing negative has happened, so there is no reason for pain. From that standpoint, from that higher consciousness, there's no pain, there's just the universe doing its own thing, and you are connected to that energy, it is part of you. Whatever your set of circumstances, they are meant to be. They are what you need to grow.

# GRATITUDE

When we are living our regular lives, we are mostly living inside of our day-to-day routines. These routines create a fog screen around us. This fog is created by various day-to-day routine emotions. Due to this fog screen, we are not able to see the beautiful things happening around us. And even when we are exiting our routines, by going on a beautiful trip or a beautiful hike, many times we are still surrounded by the fog of our routines—preventing us from appreciating the depth and quality of these beautiful moments. Therefore, many times, even when we are experiencing beautiful moments, we do not appreciate them because we are surrounded by the fog of our routine thoughts and energy.

As a consequence of this, we are used to not appreciating beautiful moments. *Gratitude* is not something we are used to doing, so we do not have any muscle memory to appreciate the beauty and blessing of a moment. We are, in essence, ungrateful for the beautiful things in our lives, and ungrateful *for* our lives.

Gratitude and appreciation are very important. When we experience beautiful things, whether they are outside our routines or part of our routines, gratitude and appreciation increase our quality of life. If we appreciate something we have, or have experienced, that something becomes more special and creates a positive effect. On the other hand, if we do not appreciate something we have or have experienced (could be a thing, a situation, or a person), then we are missing out on a significant portion of value from that thing. This is to say that we are depriving ourselves of the full value of what we have by not being grateful for it. Only when these things disappear do we start to appreciate them, because the lack creates clarity we did not have before. But it is too late at that point.

When we have an extraordinary experience, the experience might be beautiful and might bring certain levels of happiness to us, but if we would feel the feeling of gratitude to the universe on top of the normal feeling of satisfaction from the experience, the value and the satisfaction from the experience would be on a much higher level. In essence, with the same experience and the same person the value will be much higher for us if we just add the feeling of gratitude to the universe that enables us to feel and experience what we are experiencing. The meaning of this is that the lives we are already living will have much more value and much more happiness in them if we incorporate the feeling of gratitude in everything we have and everything we experience.

Another aspect is the reverse aspect. If we do not appreciate what the universe is bringing to us and we do not feel gratitude to the universe for the blessing we are receiving, the universe could stop sending us these blessings as they are not appreciated and valued by us. The universe will show us, guide us, teach us, and bring us what we need to help our growth and to help us evolve. If we do not grow and appreciate the value from the positive things we have, the people around us and the experiences we have, the universe might decide to teach us from the negative standpoint. By taking away the things, people, and experiences we have, to help us learn the lessons we need to evolve and grow. The universe will always bring us what we need to grow, so if we were not able to grow and evolve from receiving the gifts and the positive things that the universe brought us, then we might have to learn from not having, which is a much harder way to experience life. It is always much better to evolve through the positive, as life that way is a much more beautiful experience. The alternative to this type of learning is learning by suffering and no one wants that, but many unfortunately experience it.

Therefore, gratitude and appreciation have double the value. One, if we appreciate and feel gratitude, whether for a big thing or a small thing, we have increased the level of enjoyment received from that person, thing, or situation. Two, if we are ungrateful, the universe might teach us by removing these things from our lives. Surely, it is much better to evolve, learn, and develop by having and appreciating the beautiful and positive things, people, and experiences in our lives.

There are many ways to express gratitude to the universe, and each person can find their own way to do so. We can do it in the simplest ways, like noticing a beautiful day, the birds singing, or a blue sky. When we go on a hike or spend time in a park, we can notice and appreciate the beautiful trees and plants. When we are at a beach, we can be grateful for the beautiful ocean. Noticing and appreciating is gratitude, as we are not taking these things for granted.

We can do the same process with the various people in our lives, people we enjoy spending time with. People that bring positive value to our lives. We can also build a meditation routine where we note all the positive and beautiful things in our lives and how much we appreciate them. This will remind us not to take any of it for granted.

Being grateful should be developed as a muscle memory in our minds. We should train ourselves by noticing each time we are grateful, and each time we are not grateful. When we notice that we are not grateful for our lives, we can immediately think of all the positive value we have in those specific moments, so we can feel gratitude again. We can shift our mindset because it is easier to notice negative feelings when they are happening.

When we notice, we should thank the universe for letting us have gratitude in our life. The feeling of gratitude will immediately increase the enjoyment of what we are grateful for. As we practice this type of gratitude and appreciation, we can move on to appreciating smaller and smaller things in our lives, including things that are part of our daily routines. As we practice this more and more, gratitude and appreciation will become part of our muscle memory and will come naturally to us, increasing the positive value we are experiencing from the things we have and the lives we live. In turn, this brings positive feelings and energy into our lives, and increases the quality of our lives in general.

# ENERGY EFFICIENCY

Throughout our lives, we all have certain things we aim to achieve. It may be a professional goal, a successful relationship, financial objectives, or goals related to health and physique. To achieve these goals, we put forth effort. This effort is the physical effort we invest in achieving our goals as well as energetic effort. We are actually sending energy into the universe, towards what we are trying to accomplish. It starts as mental energy, and as time passes and we invest more mental energy, it manifests into the physical world. Whatever we invest our energy into, creates an energy outflow, and this outflow is needed to manifest whatever goal we are trying to achieve. As we invest more and more energy into a goal, we might feel drained of energy—literally and physically. When we invest internal energy into a specific task or idea, we convert our mental energy into a physical goal.

So far so good, but what happens when we run out of accumulated energy?

This can only happen on a physical level. Spiritually, we can tap into an endless energy source and be in a state of constant progress.

How do we *never* run out of energy? We are surrounded by the universe's boundless energy source. All we need to do is find a way to tap into that endless energy every time we need to refill our internal energy—exactly like we refill a car's gas tank. If we are open to this flow of energy all around us, it is unlimited.

Unfortunately, most people are not open to receiving the universe's energy, and their internal energy source is limited and not often replenished. To understand this concept further, consider the different types of energy we possess: mental energy (our brain's energy), physical energy (our body's energy), and source energy (the universe's energy). All are interconnected, but it's useful to differentiate between them for the sake of understanding.

Of the three types of available energy, *mental energy* is the most abundant. It feels like we can create as many thoughts as we want without any limit. But every thought created—many useless and of no real value—uses a certain amount of internal energy. When we want to achieve a specific goal and we invest a lot of mental energy into it—analysing from various angles—we feel mentally exhausted, which means we have exhausted the available energy in our mental energy tank. We can replenish this energy by rest and clearing our minds. The same applies to *physical* energy. The amounts may vary based on our physical condition, but the better our physical condition, the larger physical energy tank we have at our disposal. We can increase this energy tank by exercising and doing physical activities. The bigger the physical energy tank, the more physical activities we can do. And we replenish this energy with rest and food. Our *internal universe* energy is the one we are least aware of. This energy is similar to the universe's energy all around us. We have a drop of it inside our bodies. This energy is *source* energy and can be used to generate and replenish mental and physical energy.

Inside our bodies, we have a limited amount of source energy. But we are surrounded by the universe's energy (source energy) all the time. Therefore, if we figure out a way to connect to the abundance of energy around us, we can refill our energy tanks constantly. Like with physical and mental energies, the more we use source energy, the more we will have. The universe's energy is unlimited as long as we learn how to tap into it. Furthermore, as the universe's energy is the source energy *for everything*, we can convert this energy into mental and physical energy and increase our capacities in all three areas by doing so.

To refill our energy tanks with source energy, we need to connect our internal energy with the universe's energy. This can be done in many ways, the most popular being meditation. Meditation stops our mind's and ego's endless movement and allows our internal energy to connect with the universe. Another popular way is to be in nature. When surrounded by nature, our bodies' vibrations correlate with the energy of nature, which is correlated with the universe's energy. The moment we connect our internal energy with the energy of the universe, the universe's energy immediately starts flowing into our body and refills our energy tanks. We don't need to do anything, it just happens. All we need to do is to connect with the universe so the energy will flow.

There are many other ways to connect with the universe's energy, like the feeling of love, compassion, and certain ceremonies. Find what works for you and practice that path. When you are on the right path, you will feel recharged, like your internal energy level is charging and becoming higher. This is a sign you have found a way to connect to the universe's energy and your internal energy tanks are refilling.

The next phase is to learn how to invest the energy you have efficiently. The term *efficient*, in this context, refers to the paths you choose—whether there be several or one. When you invest your energy toward a certain goal, you need to monitor how much energy you are investing and the results. With important goals, you want to invest more energy. But in all cases, it's important to monitor the level of energy used versus the results and adjust accordingly.

For example, you might invest one pound of energy into something and only receive minute results. This might mean you are not investing your energy in the most efficient way. It would be much better to invest your one pound of energy and receive greater results. To be *energy efficient,* try a different approach. For example, if the initial way yielded 20% for every one pound of energy invested, but the second way yielded 50% for every pound invested, you have found a more productive path towards your goal.

You might choose to continue investing your energy the same way until you reach your goal or try another path that might yield 60% or 70%, allowing you to reach your goal quicker and more efficiently. Every time you invest energy towards a certain goal, monitor the amount of energy used and the success of that path. If the success is not sufficient and efficient enough, try a different path until you find the most efficient and productive way to reach your goals.

Of course, it's possible, despite trying different paths, you don't find an efficient way to reach your goals. In that case, consider adjusting your goals or search for another path to get there.

This process of monitoring your energy investment and adjusting your course accordingly will allow you to invest your energy efficiently. And, if you replenish constantly by keeping your energy tanks connected to the universe's energy, you will always have enough energy to accomplish the things you want to do. You will also live a fuller life and become a happier individual.

# THE IMPORTANCE OF NATURE

Most people are unaware that every object, person, animal, tree, flower, and city has their own energy vibration. The quality of the energy vibration depends on the quality of what or who is emitting it. For instance, a tree would have a positive energy because it is directly connected with the vibration of the universe. On the other hand, a crowded and polluted city would have a negative vibration because it is the sum of all the vibrations dwelling inside it, most on a much lower quality vibration frequency compared to the pure vibration of the universe. The energy of a city contains and is the sum of the energy of all the people inhibiting the city, who might be anxious, angry, frustrated, and stressed over their day-to-day struggles. Therefore, the vibration of a congested city is on the other side of the scale from the harmonious vibration of the universe. More than half the world's population live in urban areas.

Every person has a specific energy vibration. Our vibration is affected by many variables, but one of them is our surroundings. We might be in a place with a negative vibration, like a toxic workplace. Or, a socially negative environment, like a war zone. Our body will absorb a negative vibration frequency and adjust to vibrate on that very same level. We simply have the tendency to adjust to the vibrations of our surroundings.

Some people who are very conscious of their energy and vibration, might be able to maintain a positive vibration frequency even in a negative situation, but this is very difficult to do and only a very small minority of people can do it. Most people are not conscious they even emit and absorb vibrations and are not conscious of keeping and maintaining their vibration on a high level.

This process is not a conscious decision for most people. It happens in the background. If you go to a place that has a high level of conflict, where there is aggression, congestion, and negativity, you will start feeling discomfort and your vibration frequency will drop. That discomfort is really your energy vibrations struggling to feel comfortable in a low energy frequency environment. This, in turn, creates the feeling of discomfort. It is a negative feeling, so if, after feeling this discomfort, you exit the negative energy zone, or work hard to maintain your vibration frequency despite being in a lower energy zone, you will restore your energy to a higher level. You'll know you were successful when you no longer feel the discomfort of the lower energy vibration, and you experience a positive sensation.

But be careful. If you are not able to leave the lower energy zone and can't work on your energy field to keep it separated from the lower energy vibration around you, you will become accustomed to the negative energy around you, adapting to it, and adjusting your frequency to the lower and more negative level of vibration. The big problem in this case is that you will not feel the discomfort of the negative energy anymore, because your body has adopted the lower frequency and got used to it. The only indication of this occurring is that you will a background negative feeling, but most people are used to living their lives in this type of environment, and therefore will not be sensitive to this. Another indicator of this situation is when you move to a higher vibration and feel a sudden positive sensation. Your body feels a jolt of the universe's pure energy and recognizes it. You'll feel at ease in this natural vibration state, even if it is temporary. This is exactly what happens when we spend time in nature.

Spend time in nature. Spend time in the mountains, next to water, in a forest, in fields, or in the desert. The type of nature you're exposed to is not important. While people have different preferences, enjoying a variety of natural environments, what is important is finding the time to be close to nature. Trees, rocks, water, sand, sky, and grass are directly connected to the energy vibration of the universe. They emit positive vibrations into their surroundings.

As you spend time in nature, your body will absorb the natural vibration of the universe, become one with it, and automatically adjust your vibration to the higher level. The side effect of this is a feeling of comfort. But there are much deeper benefits. When your molecules adjust to natural energy vibrations, all the cells in your body undergo a virtual healing process. The more time you spend in nature, the more significant the healing process and the healthier you will feel.

There are many factors that will affect the level and speed your cells will readjust to the natural vibration of the universe, but the basic are:

1. The more time you spend in nature, the better you will feel.

2. The purer the natural environment, the more positive the effect. For example, a forest or mountain with only a few people around you will affect you more powerfully than a very crowded beach, which has the sum of the energies of all the people around you.

3. By being in nature, your cells will automatically adjust to the vibration of nature and the universe. The more conscious you are of this process, the faster and the more significant the adjustment will be.

It doesn't matter what activity you choose, whether it's hiking, biking, resting, picnics, boating, surfing, sports, or fishing, the important thing is that you take time from your busy life to spend time in nature. Allow your body to adjust and heal from urban life. Connect to the natural vibration of the universe and increase your quality of life by increasing the quality of your vibration frequency.

# SPA FOR THE SOUL – MEDITATION

Everyone feels anxious about certain things happening in their lives. It is that uncomfortable feeling that hovers in the background, like anxiety, fear, anger, sadness, discomfort, or any other negative emotion that most people experience in their daily lives. This is where meditation comes into play. The purpose of meditation is to disconnect ourselves from the daily negative thought-loops that our egos are running in our minds, and instead to connect our souls to the beautiful and harmonious energy of the universe.

Understanding meditation is simple. All we need to do is to stop your thoughts and clear our minds. We need to stop our egos from generating the circular routine of negative thoughts that in turn generate the negative emotions mentioned above. While understanding meditation is easy, it can be hard to execute. Stopping our thoughts is not that easy to do. We are used to engaging in continuous thoughts loops regarding potential future negative events and worries or past negative events. The ego keeps running these thoughts in a circular pattern, again and again. These negative thoughts generate negative emotions. While it is clear why you would want to stop this circular negative thought process, it's not clear how to do so.

There are thousands of meditation techniques; many developed over thousands of years. As humans, have been suffering from the same issues since inception. A common thread of all meditation techniques is stillness. We need to remain still for our egos to clear your mind. We need to stop our mind from wandering, thinking about things that make us anxious. While it is hard to focus, and many people feel that meditation is just something they need to force themselves to do, practice makes perfect.

We can treat meditation like a spa for your mind and soul. Doing meditation is like going to a spa of energy and light. When we find this feeling during meditation, it will feel as if our mind is going to a spa. The feeling is like receiving a massage or a relaxing spa treatment. The feeling will be relaxing, and we will notice that we are connected with the energy of the universe as opposed to the energy of our thoughts. This way of looking at meditation will help us understand that meditation is not something we need to suffer through to get to a better place and a better feeling. It's an enjoyable relaxation place where we can transform our minds. Enjoy the process and you will experience positive benefits the same way you are enjoying a spa or massage treatment and experience the positive results.

First, to help you start meditating, instead of pushing yourself to meditate, think about the positive sensation of going to a spa for your mind and soul. That is an incentive to start meditating. Then, when you start, think about relaxing. Connect your energy to the energy of the universe and focus on the beautiful energy flowing through you. That is an amazing incentive to do meditation. Every time you feel anxiety, anger, distress, or any other feeling of discomfort, go to the spa for the mind and soul. Relax, breathe, rejuvenate, and then you go back to doing whatever physical things you need to.

In the beginning, it will be hard to control your thoughts. You have been thinking the same thoughts all your life, and it's hard to change. But as you practice meditation, you will get better and more competent at it. As you get better, you will be able to control your thoughts for longer periods of time, and therefore do longer meditations. You will also be able to connect more and more with your higher consciousness and the energy of the universe and receive and replenish your body's energy reserves.

My daily routine consists of three meditations. The first one is a gratitude meditation I do in the shower. During my morning shower, I close my eyes and send gratitude to the universe. I thank my higher consciousness for all the blessings I have in my life. You can make a list of all the things you are grateful for, like health, resources, a good workplace, family, a connection to the energy of the universe, etc. I go through all the blessings I have in my life, in their order of importance, starting with my connection to the universe and my higher consciousness. The purpose of this process is to remind myself of all the positive things in my life. This is important for several reasons. First, gratitude for all the amazing things I have in my life counterbalances any negative thoughts and emotions my mind might have generated. Second, the connection with the universe energy through gratitude, aligns my vibration frequency with the vibration of the universe. Third, this exercise creates a positive muscle memory to start each day with positive energy and vibration.

Meditation establishes the connection to the universe's energy and your higher consciousness, which allows us to operate on a higher vibrational level.

The last part of my shower meditation is to connect the physical body to the energy of the universe in order to vitalize the body itself and bring the beautiful health energy into the physical body and clean it from it any negative sickness energy before it manifests as a physical illness. From a technical aspect, this meditation does not need to be done in a shower, it could be done anywhere. For me it works best in a shower, but the most important technical aspect of this meditation is that it's the first thing that I do in the mornings. This aligns my energy with the positive energy of the universe before the day starts and the day-to-thoughts take over.

The second meditation I do comes in the morning as well, before I start the tasks and the routines of the day. In this meditation I sit in a comfortable place, in a meditation pose and close my eyes. I start focusing on my breathing and clearing my mind. Then I transcend my consciousness to my higher consciousness on a higher plane. The purpose of this meditation is to connect directly with my higher consciousness. It's important to note that I have been practicing meditation for over twenty years and it took me a lot of practice to be able to accomplish this type of connection. Therefore, it might work or might not work for you, but the important part of this meditation, is to be able to clear your mind of your routine thoughts and look for a connection to your higher consciousness and energy. The more you practice the better connection you will feel and the higher you will be able to reach. The purpose of this meditation is to remind us that we are "spiritual beings having a temporary human experience". Connecting with the vast higher consciousness, which is us as the spiritual being, puts the small physical things in our small physical world in its proper perspective.

The third meditation is before going to sleep, while I am in bed. I try to connect to my higher consciousness and higher energy, in order to clear the mind from the routine daily thoughts that have been inhabiting the mind during the day. This is back to the concept of bringing your mind and soul back to the spa just before I fall asleep. It will allow me to fall asleep faster and have a better sleep free of all the negative and routine thoughts that my mind and ego have been running during the day.

Common threads in all meditations are:

1. Stop the thought-loops running in your mind.
2. Establish and feel the connection with the universe's energy.
3. Replenish your positive energy tanks.
4. Connect to your soul by centering yourself and finding your internal happiness.
5. Find your internal balance and harmony.
6. Remember you are a spiritual being having a temporary human experience.
7. Be connected, healthy, and *happy*.

# ACKNOWLEDGEMENTS

I would like to express special gratitude to my brother, E, who has been sharing the path with me since inception. E has been my partner in business and in life. He's been a teacher and a fellow traveler.

I want to also thank my teachers, Aaliyah and others who helped me understand the knowledge that has been accumulated and developed over thousands of years in philosophies such as Buddhism, Taoism, Stoicism, Tantra, yoga, and others.

I also want to thank life partners I have shared parts of my journey with. Through all of them, I learned a lot—even when I was the teacher. Every connection opened a new energy source that allowed wisdom to enter my life.

I want to thank Lizzie, Lana, Audrey and Erika for helping with this book. And to the many others who helped and inspired the creation of this book, I appreciate your assistance.

During this journey, I met many teachers in the form of spiritual guides, business partners, lovers, and friends. Some people shared my path for a while, and some have shared the journey for many years. To all the souls who entered my life, I am grateful.

Printed in Great Britain
by Amazon

48914890R00098